CW00953024

Challenges to Democracy in the 21st Century

Series Editor
Hanspeter Kriesi, Department of Political and Social Science
European University Institute, San Domenico Di Fiesole, Firenze, Italy

Democracy faces substantial challenges as we move into the 21st Century. The West faces malaise; multi-level governance structures pose democratic challenges; and the path of democratization rarely runs smoothly. This series examines democracy across the full range of these contemporary conditions. It publishes innovative research on established democracies, democratizing polities and democracy in multi-level governance structures. The series seeks to break down artificial divisions between different disciplines, by simultaneously drawing on political communication, comparative politics, international relations, political theory, and political economy.

More information about this series at
http://www.palgrave.com/gp/series/14889

Richard Rose

How Sick Is British Democracy?

A Clinical Analysis

Richard Rose
Government and Public Policy
University of Strathclyde
Glasgow, UK

Challenges to Democracy in the 21st Century
ISBN 978-3-030-73122-9   ISBN 978-3-030-73123-6   (eBook)
https://doi.org/10.1007/978-3-030-73123-6

This Palgrave Macmillan imprint is published by the registered company Springer Nature
Switzerland AG
The registered company address is: Gewerbestrasse 11, 6330 Cham, Switzerland

To my wife, Rosemary, and her parents James A. and Clare Amberton Kenny.

Preface

The Need for Clinical Analysis

Even though the body politic does not have a limited life, a flood of books claims that democracy is dying. Authors who celebrated the freedom gained by tens of millions when the Berlin Wall fell now lament what has happened since. In *The Twilight of Democracy*, Anne Applebaum (2020) writes, 'any society can turn against democracy. Indeed, if history is anything to go by, all of our societies eventually will'. For some social scientists the global economic collapse of 2008 triggered the *Crises of Democracy* (Przeworski 2019). The rise of populist parties is interpreted as creating the paradoxical threat of *The People vs. Democracy* (Mounk 2018). Within two years of Donald Trump entering the White House in succession to Barack Obama, two Harvard professors authored a post-mortem about *How Democracies Die* (Levitsky and Ziblatt 2018). A Cambridge University professor has gone further, explaining *How Democracy Ends* (Runciman 2018).

The durability of Britain's democratic institutions does not mean they are immune to symptoms of ill health. Popular distrust in parties and Parliament is today greater than distrust in any other major institution of British society. The Conservative government has gone through three prime ministers in five years, and the Labour party fought the last two elections under a leader that most Labour MPs considered unfit to be prime minister. In the 2016 referendum on European Union membership, the majority of Britons rejected their leaders' consensus about Europe and voted to leave the EU. The Constitution Unit's (2020) detailed review of government practices asks, 'Are we heading for a democratic lockdown?' A leading Conservative minister, Michael Gove (2020), has invoked the Italian Marxist theorist Antonio Gramsci to describe 'morbid symptoms' in the British government that require radical reform, and former Prime Minister Gordon Brown (2021) warns that the United Kingdom is at risk of becoming 'a failed state'.

Generalizations about the death of democracy are often supported by reference to the replacement of elected governments by dictators in Europe in the 1920s and 1930s, such as the death of the Weimar Republic in Germany and its succession by Hitler's Third Reich. They overlook the fact that the democracies that died did so in their youth. Similarly, in the successor states of the Soviet Union, democracy was aborted or died shortly after birth. None was a long-established democracy like the United Kingdom or the United States.

The claim that democracy is dying is a forecast about the end point in an as yet incomplete process of political change. Social science theories provide a means of forecasting future events from available evidence. Mounk (2018) draws on theories of economic stagnation, identity conflict and social media threat to forecast democracy in danger. Mounk cites the election of Donald Trump as president as a potentially fatal threat to democracy, and Trump's reaction to his election defeat in 2020 was a real threat to American democracy. However, the inauguration of President Joseph Biden fits the theory that the institutions of American democracy are strong enough to check those who abuse their power, a theory developed to account for the removal of Richard Nixon from the White House in 1974.

The variety of political systems described as threatened with death indicates that British democracy is not alone in facing challenges to its political health. However, this book rejects the facile generalization that whatever happens in another country today will happen in Britain tomorrow. A generalization drawn from populist parties gaining power in Italy in 2017 can be refuted by the meteoric fall of the populist Brexit parties of Nigel Farage in Britain. The ability of an undemocratic party to win a significant number of seats in the German parliament has shown the resilience of democratic institutions: the Alternative for Germany (AfD) is treated as a pariah, ostracized when German parties form a coalition government.

When a Finnish populist party was co-opted into government, it demonstrated that participating in government is a threat to populists, for the party split rather than face up to the demands of government.

The statistical analyses of political systems globally, like that of public health during the coronavirus crisis, can only provide statements of probabilities. Like a doctor's examination of an individual patient, clinical analysis of the health of democracy in a single country has the advantage of being able to take into account evidence specific to its history and political institutions. To paraphrase Tolstoy's epigram about families, 'Among unhealthy democracies, each is unhealthy in its own way'. Evaluating British democracy within a national context avoids concluding from a comparison with the putative virtues of other countries that British democracy would be healthier if it wasn't British. However, this does not mean that just because political institutions and actions are British they are necessarily healthy.

Britain meets the minimum requirements for a democratic political system. Everyone can vote in free elections in which parties compete to take control of government by offering a choice of policies and candidates. Democratic political systems are resilient; the government of the day is accountable to the electorate for how it has governed, and voters periodically can re-elect it or eject it from office (Schumpeter 1952).

A democratic election inevitably shows that more than half of the voters have voted for losing parties. In a healthy democracy, losers consent to the outcome of a free and fair ballot and can try to reverse the outcome at a subsequent election. Donald Trump's refusal to give consent to his defeat earned him an unprecedented second impeachment by Congress for inciting an insurrection.

Just because democratic institutions offer people the chance to vote for what they want, this does not mean that all of the policies of a democratically elected government will be effective. Democratic institutions cannot guarantee a high rate of economic growth nor can they prevent infection and death during the coronavirus pandemic. Democracy and effectiveness can be combined in four different ways. A government can be democratic and effective, as happens in Scandinavia, or it can be undemocratic and ineffective, as in Belarus. The political institutions of Singapore are effective in managing the results of undemocratic elections as well as managing the economy. Mediterranean countries such as Italy and Greece have democratic political systems but ineffective governments.

Democratic institutions do need to be effective in curbing the potential excesses of politicians who win elections. The authors of the American Constitution put their trust in political institutions rather than in virtuous and trustworthy politicians. As James Madison, one of the authors of the American Constitution, explained in *The Federalist Papers* Number 51:

> If men were angels, no government would be necessary. If angels were to govern men, neither external nor internal controls on government would be necessary. In framing a government which is to be administered by men over men, the great difficulty lies in this: you must first enable the government to control the governed; and in the next place oblige it to control itself.

British democracy is healthy to the extent that its political institutions are strong enough to curb any behaviour by self-interested politicians that would be damaging to the institutions and rights of the people they represent.

This book's purpose is to give a clinical diagnosis of the British body politic in order to identify which democratic institutions are functioning as they should and which are not. Without examining systematically the vital institutions of the British government, discussions of the state of democracy in the abstract and claims that it is threatened with death are rhetorically strong but weak on evidence. The focus on the institutions of governance complements studies of the ineffectiveness and blunders of the British government that democracy may correct but cannot prevent.

The health of the democratic body politic depends first of all on the behaviour of its governors. The response of Whigs and Tories to demands for democratization in the nineteenth century laid the foundations of a political system robust enough to withstand the challenges of war and economic depression in the twentieth century. The Second World War ended with Britain's democratic institutions intact. Since then, world crises have been rhetorically invoked dozens of times to describe major policy challenges, whether recurring, such as the weakness of the pound, or unique, such as the coronavirus pandemic. However, none has resulted in the disablement or death of British democracy. The institutions that Winston Churchill and Clement Attlee passed on to their successors have adapted to change; they have not been repudiated by an elite coup or a populist uprising like those occurring in fledgling and aborted democracies elsewhere in the world.

Diagnosis comes before prescription. Patients who go to a doctor usually have a perception that something is wrong with them, but doctors do not jump to conclusions from their patient's self-diagnosis. Nor should political scientists confuse the perceptions of democracy that people report in surveys with evidence provided by a hands-on examination of the political institutions of the body politic which offer a portrait of British democracy warts and all. A discriminating examination avoids the mistake of judging the whole of the body politic by a single part. It can identify those institutions that are in good political health and those that are not. The clinical diagnosis does not produce a simplistic finding of a democracy in perfect health or in a dire state. Nor does it generalize from a single event, whether it is victory in the Falklands War or Brexit.

Since the health of British democracy tends to fluctuate up and down, the time span of analysis affects the diagnosis. At the end of the Second World War, Britain was a great power abroad and building welfare state institutions at home offering womb-to-tomb benefits. A decade later the abortive Suez War put paid to its great power status, and the economic dynamic of reconstructed European democracies led to books with titles such as *Suicide of a Nation* (Koestler 1963). In February 1974 a confrontation between the government and trade unions and a global economic recession brought warnings that an overloaded British government was going politically bankrupt. British institutions and citizens responded democratically, electing a new government with Margaret Thatcher as prime minister. She gave the economy a dose of free-market economics, a cure that some thought worse than the sickness.

This book focuses on the state of British politics in the past quarter-century, a period long enough to provide substantial evidence but not so long as to confound conclusions by relying on evidence when times were different. When Tony Blair entered Downing Street in 1997 he created a feel-good mood about British democracy; that had gone before the end of 13 years of Labour government. Since 2010, voters have shown varying degrees of confidence in Conservative governments in four successive elections.

Having a political system that has the essential characteristics of democracy—free competitive elections that determine control of government and that can hold the government to account—does not ensure that it is always in perfect health. Since the health of the body politic, like that of individuals, is not constant over decades, it is important to differentiate the frequency with which a symptom of ill health occurs. British democracy is in good health as long as deviations from perfect health are infrequent, such as a referendum rejecting the recommendation of the government of the day, or recur intermittently, such as more people disapproving the performance of a prime minister rather than giving approval. If a condition is long-lasting, such as the governing party never winning as much as half the vote and losing parties sometimes getting as much as two-thirds of the total vote, the persistence of this symptom indicates that it is not fatal.

The first chapter makes clear the procedures this book uses to evaluate the health of British democracy. Because democracy has many definitions, some widely agreed and others that are partisan, the chapter sets out a model of the anatomy of a perfectly healthy body politic. This is used to identify minor or potentially fatal symptoms of ill health during the past quarter-century.

Voters choosing the government of the day is at the heart of democratic government. Chapter 2 examines how the British electoral system enables voters to know which party to hold accountable for government by reducing the effective choice to the democratic minimum of the governing party and the Loyal Opposition. The health of democracy depends upon the governing parties adapting to changes in society and voters being ready to change their vote if the party they usually support fails to change. The Conservative and Labour parties have alternated in government for almost a century because each has shown a healthy ability to adapt to changing generations of voters.

Parties are the lifeblood of democratic government. Chapter 3 explains how parties nominate the candidates who become MPs; the majority party's MPs are the pool from which government ministers are drawn; and party whips determine how MPs vote. In addition to representing parties, MPs collectively present a greater diversity of faces and voices than ever before in their gender, race and ethnic origins. However, the immurement of MPs and political journalists in the Palace of Westminster creates a political elite more responsive to each other than to the concerns of ordinary people.

The prime minister is the leader of a political party as well as the British government. Chapter 4 emphasizes that the political health of a prime minister depends on their being an electoral asset and leading an effective government. To enter Downing Street a politician must first be elected party leader by the party's MPs and party members. Once in government office, the leader is challenged to make a small number of major decisions, such as striking a balance between the threat of coronavirus to the country's health and to its economy. He or she must also retain the electoral support necessary to re-elect the government. While the personality of prime ministers such as Margaret Thatcher and Tony Blair remained relatively constant, opinion polls and election results show that their political health fluctuated throughout their time in Downing Street.

Even though the ship of state has only one tiller, many hands are involved in steering it, as Chapter 5 documents. Cabinet ministers have the legitimacy to decide what their department ought to do, but their career in party politics is often no preparation for giving direction to a large and complex government department. Ministers are supported by senior civil servants who are experienced in turning political promises into government policies. Civil servants welcome ministers who want to promote the department and their careers as long as they do not insist on policies that make good soundbites but are likely to crash on the rocks. Ministers also rely on political advisers and experts for help in achieving success. The multiplicity of those involved in the policy process helps ministers reshuffle blame and dodge accountability for departmental failures.

To describe the body politic of the United Kingdom of Great Britain and Northern Ireland as a nation-state is misleading. It is multinational state. Chapter 6 shows that citizens do not identify themselves as UKs, but as English, Scots, Welsh, Irish or British. Nor is the United Kingdom a state with fixed boundaries; it is a kingdom with boundaries that have expanded and shrunk as a consequence of battles and inheritance. Being a multinational state is no obstacle to democracy, as Switzerland shows, but disunity about the boundaries of the state is a symptom of ill health. The Scottish National Party wants Scotland to be an independent state and Sinn Fein ministers in the Northern Ireland government want it to be part of another state, the Republic of Ireland.

If a democratic government is not to abuse its powers, courts must have the authority to say 'Stop it' to a popularly elected government that violates constitutional rules. Chapter 7 focuses on the consequences of Britain having the supreme constitutional authority, the High Court of Parliament, weak in relation to the government of the day. Thus, when disputes arise about the legitimacy of a government measure, the government of the day can be the judge of its own actions and invoke its electoral legitimacy to justify what it does. Judges have preferred to avoid getting involved in political disputes about whether the government has acted beyond the broad and vague grants of the powers of an unwritten constitution.

Although the government in Westminster likes to appear as the all-powerful head of a sovereign state, Chapter 8 shows how much it depends on a community of public bodies to deliver the policies for which it takes credit and is accountable. The community includes local and devolved government, non-elected public institutions such as the Bank of England, the National Health Service and universities. In foreign policy the United Kingdom is one island among a sea of states, some democratic and some undemocratic; each has the same claim to nominal sovereignty as Britain and their national interests place limits on what the United Kingdom can achieve. Brexit has produced a paradox: the domestic priority of bringing back power to Britain has placed fresh limits and regulations on the United Kingdom's power to trade with the European Union. When prime ministers speak of their vision of Britain's role in the world, their vision appears to reflect a mental map of the days of Empire rather than the twenty-first century.

Systematic examination of the body politic shows that some parts of British democracy are in good health while others are not, but symptoms of ill health do not appear fatal. Disagreements about how government should handle major issues such as taxation are evidence of good health, because democratic politics is about the free expression of differences of opinion. However, it is a sign of intermittent ill health if an electoral system abruptly changes how much support is enough to win control of the government. In 2005 Labour won a comfortable parliamentary majority with only 35.2% of the vote, while in 2017 the Conservatives failed to get a majority with 42.3% of the vote. It would be a potentially fatal symptom if the government of the day postponed parliamentary elections for fear it would lose office.

Symptoms of the government falling short of the democratic ideal stimulate big-bang proposals for the reform of the British government. Impossible reforms are durably attractive: advocates of proportional representation have been urging its adoption for more than a century, and the idea of turning the United Kingdom into a federal political system dates from the nineteenth century. Reforming the way in which politicians behave presents a challenge familiar to psychiatrists: patients must want to change their behaviour for a diagnosis to result in a cure. However, the principal beneficiaries of the existing system, Conservative and Labour politicians, see no need for changing the electoral system that alternatively gives each party control of the power of government without being hamstrung by partners in a coalition.

It is naive to believe that just because a problem exists there must be a solution. Some forms of ill health must be accepted as a condition of British democracy being British. Politics is the art of the possible. Chapter 9 sets out proposals for improving the health of British democracy that a governing party could implement. For example, ministers could get a stronger grip on their department if the prime minister reduced the frequency of Cabinet reshuffles, and civil servants could get a better understanding of the impact of Whitehall on British society if they had a mid-career break working in local government, for not-for-profit organizations or profit-making enterprises.

Unlike the coronavirus pandemic, none of the ills of British democracy is life-threatening. They support Winston Churchill's argument: 'No one pretends that democracy is perfect or all wise. Indeed, it has been said that democracy is the worst form of government, except all those other forms that have been tried from time to time'. The commitment of Britain's governors and citizens to democracy explains why the economic depression of the 1930s did not result in the triumph of a fascist or communist movement. Instead, it produced the biggest parliamentary majority that the Conservative party has ever won. I doubt that statistics showing the extent of economic inequality today will lead to political upheavals that were not produced by inequalities of social class that persisted until the 1960s. Nor is the resilience of British democracy unique to Britain. A major review of challenges to democracy in Europe today concludes that there is 'reason for concern but no reason to dramatize' (Kriesi 2020: 237).

The ills set out in this book illustrate the perennial wisdom of Adam Smith's maxim, 'There is a great deal of ruin in a nation'. If the United Kingdom lost its hold on Northern Ireland, a number of MPs in all parties would regard this as beneficial, the removal of a troublesome political appendix. If a Scottish independencereferendum put an end to Great Britain, withdrawal would have a much bigger impact in Scotland than in England, which had its own Parliament for five centuries before the absorption of the Scottish Parliament by the Westminster Parliament created Great Britain.

When I started researching British politics in 1953, Winston Churchill was prime minister, The Times did not put news on its front page, and the BBC did not put politics in its news. While there were differences about which party ought to govern, there was no question of the health of British democracy. I have always approached British politics by systematic diagnosis because I had no knowledge of British politics when I became a graduate student at the London School of Economics and because my American education as a historian and fact-oriented Pulitzer journalist made me sceptical of abstract theories leading to grand generalizations.

Because this book concerns important issues of public policy, it is written in language suited to a broad audience. It combines concepts and evidence from the literature of political science with apposite examples from the practice of British politics. Each chapter's references note sources of evidence, and there is a guide to printed and Internet sources at the end. To include a review of the contemporary literature of democracy would have made this book as long as my 525-page doctoral thesis. It would also distract attention from the critical question that this book addresses: What is the health of British democracy today?

Glasgow, UK   Richard Rose
February 2021

REFERENCES

Applebaum, Anne. 2020. *The Twilight of Democracy*. London: Allen Lane.
Brown, Gordon. 2021. The PM's Choice Is Between a Modern Reformed UK and a Failed State. *Daily Telegraph*, January 25.
Constitution Unit 2020. *Democratic Lockdown? Monitor No. 76*, November. London: University College.
Gove, Michael. 2020. The Privilege of Public Service. https://www.ditchley.com/programme/past-events/2020/ditchley-foundation-annual-lecture-lvi.
Koestler, Arthur. 1963. *Suicide of a Nation*. London: Hutchinson.
Kriesi, Hanspeter. 2020. Is There a Crisis of Democracy in Europe? *Politische Vierteljahresschrift* 61: 237260.
Levitsky, Steven, and D. Ziblatt. 2018. *How Democracies Die*. New York: Crown.
Mounk, Yascha. 2018. *The People vs. Democracy: Why Our Freedom Is in Danger and How to Save It*. Cambridge, MA: Harvard University Press.
Przeworski, Adam. 2019. *Crises of Democracy*. New York: Cambridge University Press.
Runciman, David. 2019. *How Democracy Ends*. London: Profile Books.
Schumpeter, Joseph A. 1952. *Capitalism, Socialism and Democracy*. London: George Allen & Unwin.

ACKNOWLEDGEMENTS

As this book was written entirely during lockdown, it is up-to-date but I was unable to present ideas at planned lectures. The originally intended conversational style has been retained. Particularly detailed and helpful comments were received from Dennis Kavanagh, Kenneth Newton, Edward Page, Donley Studlar and Frank Vibert. Karen Anderson applied a sharp eye when copyediting and Natalie Wilson helped speed the book to publication. At a time when some universities define research as getting grants without regard to whether it leads to results worth publishing as a book, this is a contrarian book. It was produced without any external grant as part of my normal activity as a research professor at the University of Strathclyde.

PRAISE FOR *HOW SICK IS BRITISH DEMOCRACY?*

"This book by a world-renowned political scientist with great knowledge of the subject tackles the controversial topic of the current state of British democracy. You may not agree with all he says (I didn't), but you will certainly learn a lot (I did)."

—Kenneth Newton, *former Executive Director, European Consortium for Political Research*

"A distinguished political scientist draws upon a lifetime's work to diagnose what ails British democracy and how it can be fixed. Since the same problems surface elsewhere, this insightful and witty book is both relevant and interesting to an international audience."

—James Curran, *Professor of Communications, Goldsmiths University of London, UK*

"*How Sick Is British Democracy?* is a highly readable and sophisticated analysis of the health of British democracy. Rose deftly diagnoses the aspects of the British body politic that are struggling to retain their democratic qualities, those that are healthy, and those suffering chronic shortcomings. Students will value this extensive treatment of the institutions and practices of British democracy and be challenged to consider proposals to improve them."

—Janet Laible, *Executive Director British Politics Group, an affiliate of the American Political Science Association*

"We are used to discussing the health of the economy, but this stimulating book applies the medical analogy to British democracy. What comes across from this much needed health check is a sense of an accumulation of co-morbidities. However, the prognosis is nonetheless optimistic thanks to a detailed analysis of how UK democracy can reform itself. Like a good doctor, Richard Rose thus explains that there are no miracle cures and that the key to good health is following the right advice."

—Andrew Glencross, *Senior Lecturer in Politics, Aston University, UK*

"Richard Rose provides a thorough analysis of the state of British democracy after years of upheaval. He reports that it is in mixed health—better than fatalists would argue but not without its problems. His proposed solutions outline the terrain over which British politics will progress for years to come."

—Kevin Hickson, *Senior Lecturer in Politics, University of Liverpool, UK*

About This Book

Forecasts of the death of democracy are often heard, and the United Kingdom is included. The forecasts are based on speculative theories and selected examples drawn from countries that have never been established democracies as is Britain. This book is different: it presents a clinical analysis of the health of British democracy from the time Tony Blair arrived in Downing Street to the challenges of Brexit and the coronavirus pandemic. It systematically examines different parts of the body politic from the prime minister at the head to the limbs of a Disunited Kingdom. It finds some symptoms of ill health that are intermittent, such as the failure of parties to choose leaders who can take charge of government and win elections, while other symptoms are chronic, such as the tendency of ministers to avoid accountability when things go wrong. By comparison with the death of democracies in Europe's past, none of the British symptoms is fatal. Some symptoms can be treated by effective remedies while placebos may give the government a short-term respite from criticism. Prescriptions drawing on foreign examples such as federalism and proportional representation are perennially popular; they are also politically impossible. Being a healthy democracy does not promise effectiveness in dealing with a country's economic problems. A country can have a healthy democracy without being economically effective or, like the United States under Donald Trump, have a healthy economy while democracy is sick. Notwithstanding symptoms of ill health, Britons do not want to trade the freedom that comes with democracy for the promises made by populist and authoritarian leaders and parties.

CONTENTS

About the Author

Professor Richard Rose has pioneered innovative studies of British politics for more than half a century, beginning with *Politics in England, Governing without Consensus: an Irish Perspective* and *Understanding the United Kingdom*. Comparative research has covered parties, elections and public policy across Europe, the United States and developing countries. Immediately after the Berlin Wall fell, Rose launched the New Democracies Barometer surveys of Eastern Europe and Russia to show what happens when undemocratic regimes fall; see *Democracy and Its Alternatives* and *Understanding Post-Communist Transformation*. Richard Rose has given seminars in 45 countries and research has been translated into 18 languages. He is professor of public policy at the University of Strathclyde Glasgow and holds visiting appointments at the Robert Schuman Centre of the European University Institute Florence and the Science Centre Berlin.

LIST OF FIGURES

LIST OF TABLES

CHAPTER 1

Diagnosing the Health of the Body Politic

When diagnosing an individual's health, a medical doctor has in mind the anatomy of a perfectly healthy body. Comparing this ideal-type model with the results of a clinical examination of a patient enables a doctor to assess whether the patient is in good health or whether there are any symptoms of ill health. This book uses a similar method to evaluate whether and in what ways British democracy is sick (Etzioni 1985; Likierman 2020).

In this book, the health of democracy is diagnosed by examining the anatomy of the British body politic and comparing the results with a model of a perfectly healthy democracy. Although the United Kingdom is a unitary state, its institutional anatomy is complex. Its central organs are in Westminster, a collective noun describing the institutions that cluster around Whitehall and Parliament Square, while its limbs extend throughout the United Kingdom. Elected politicians head some institutions, while others are headed by persons appointed by ministers or recruited on the basis of professional qualifications and expertise.

Anatomizing the democratic body politic differs from studies of political systems that reduce their complex characteristics to a single number. However, numbers such as 94 or 86, the scores of the United Kingdom and the United States on the Freedom House Index, have no intrinsic meaning (https://freedomhouse.org/countries/freedom-world/scores).

© The Author(s), under exclusive license to Springer Nature Switzerland AG 2021
R. Rose, *How Sick Is British Democracy?*
Challenges to Democracy in the 21st Century,
https://doi.org/10.1007/978-3-030-73123-6_1

The Index groups countries according to their labels into three descriptive categories: free, partly free or unfree. However, because the democratic body politic has many attributes, shorthand labels cannot identify which particular parts of the body politic are healthy and which are not. Britain scores the same on the Index as seven other countries, including Estonia and Germany, but this does not mean that the condition of British democracy is the same as theirs. Nor does it mean that Belize, with the same Index score as the United States, is governed in the same way as America. Just as a doctor learns more about the health of particular patients by examining one patient at a time, so a political scientist can learn more about the political health of a given country by examining it in detail rather than drawing inferences from a single statistic giving a global ranking.

Public opinion surveys frequently ask people how satisfied they are with the way that democracy is working in Britain. Since the question was first put in the mid-1970s, Britons have divided into three groups—satisfied, dissatisfied and don't know. Sometimes those expressing satisfaction are in the majority or plurality; sometimes the dissatisfied are the most numerous; and often people with no opinion are the median group. Since attitudes have fluctuated over the years, there are periods in which those satisfied have been increasing, such as the 1980s, and periods when the dissatisfied have been increasing, such as the past few years. However, there is no significant long-term trend (Kaase and Newton 1996: 62; Centre for the Future of Democracy 2020: Fig. 15).

While survey data can be used to test hypotheses about why people differ in their perceptions of government, the relationship between perceptions and political institutions is problematic. Perceptions are not the same as what is perceived; they are impressions that individuals have about politics. Because perceptions are subjective judgements of individuals, they can reflect an individual's partisan commitment or their limited knowledge of government. Doctors do not diagnose a patient's health based on a patient's perception of what is wrong with themselves. Instead, the doctor makes a hands-on examination of the patient in search of symptoms of the cause of their problem.

The emphasis on how British political institutions work provides better evidence for evaluating the democratic health of the body politic than inferences drawn from theories that forecast the collapse of democracy in future. While non-Marxist as well as Marxist theories may forecast that economic recession threatens the life of democracy, the reaction of

Western democracies to the recessions of 1975 and 2008 is evidence of democratic resilience (see Rose and Peters 1978; Wolinetz and Zaslove 2018). Social psychological theories that assume a common identity is necessary to maintain a democratic political system have been rejected by the persistence of many multinational democracies, including the United Kingdom, founded in 1801, and the Confederation of Switzerland, created in 1848.

Since human bodies do not always function as they should, it is important to distinguish minor symptoms, for example, a fall in voter turnout, from a major symptom, such as a big vote for an undemocratic party. It is unreasonable to treat as a permanent disability occasional departures from perfect health, such as the Labour party choosing a leader that most Labour MPs thought unfit for Downing Street or to assume that the next Conservative prime minister will have the same character as Boris Johnson.

This chapter clarifies the many ways in which democracy is defined in the abstract and relates this to an examination of the British body politic in perfect health and to symptoms of bad health. The British body politic is in good health as long as departures from the model of perfect health are intermittent rather than chronic, and persisting ailments are minor handicaps rather than potentially fatal.

1.1   Democracy: A Disembodied Ideal

Democracy is an abstract concept that refers to a particular type of political system that is a global ideal. Freedom House describes many countries that hold elections and describe themselves as democratic as falling far short of the democratic ideal. The median country in the world today is neither a totally authoritarian regime, nor is it a failed democracy because most countries have never been governed democratically.

While there tends to be a consensus among doctors about what defines good health, this is not the case with democracy. Ancient Greek philosophers such as Aristotle and Polybius defined democracy as rule by the people, but considered it a threat to healthy government. They feared a popular majority would substitute mob rule for good government. The definition of the people has changed greatly over time. The American Constitution defined a slave as three-fifths of a person for the purpose of allocating seats in Congress, Britain did not allow women to vote until 1918 and Switzerland did not do so until 1971.

Because democracy is a positive symbol, it is used and abused in many ways. A 1997 study by David Collier and Steven Levitsky found more than 500 different examples of democracy with adjectives and two decades later Jean-Paul Gagnon (2018) catalogued 2234 examples of democracy with adjectives. The name of the country is often added to take into account characteristics of its political system, as in such phrases as British democracy or American democracy. Adding an adjective can stretch the meaning of democracy or even turn it inside out. The Soviet Union did so, describing its satellite states as people's democracies. The constitution of North Korea officially describes its totalitarian regime as the Democratic People's Republic of Korea, and Mao Zedong incorporated the term people's democratic dictatorship in the constitution of the People's Republic of China.

Democracy can be used to give symbolic appeal to partisan institutions. The Labour party has always described itself as having a democratic structure, but its governing body, the National Executive Committee, is corporatist. It represents the party's stakeholders rather than individuals: the trade unions, the parliamentary Labour party and constituency parties, and there are single seats reserved for socialist societies, youth, Scotland and Wales. In the United States the term liberal democracy reflects political values favoured by supporters of one wing of the Democratic Party. The alternative to liberal democracy is a Conservative democracy. However, when I ask friends who are liberal democrats what the alternative to liberal democracy is, the answer usually is: authoritarianism. The chief Wikipedia entry for Conservative democracy describes it as a term invented by Turkish leader Recep Erdogan to describe an Islamic form of democracy.

Abraham Lincoln's description of American government as 'government by the people, for the people and of the people' provides a succinct and rhetorically powerful definition of the ideal democracy. But when you try to apply these three terms to an existing government, whether American or British, lots of problems arise.

Government by the people is literally impossible in any political system larger than a village. Political leaders rhetorically claim that they speak for all the people in order to marginalize their opponents. When a referendum gives voters the power to decide an issue, the people speak with two voices, as in the Brexit vote on whether to leave or remain in the European Union. When voters elect a parliament, up to half a dozen parties win seats enabling them to speak for some people. The British electoral system is designed to convert a minority of the popular vote into a parliamentary majority. In American presidential elections since 1960, the electoral college has awarded the presidency to John F. Kennedy, Richard Nixon, Bill Clinton, George W. Bush and Donald Trump even though each won less than half the popular vote, and Bush and Trump became president even though each finished second in the popular vote.

Governing for the people is sometimes interpreted as governing in the public interest, that is, for the good of all citizens. This positive term is contrasted with governing on behalf of narrow interests. However, the assumption that all citizens agree on their interests is contrary to the idea that democratic politics is a process for articulating and reconciling different interests in society. There was no consensus on either side of the Atlantic that fighting a war in Iraq was in the public interest. Nor is there a consensus about what laws are appropriate to protect or advance the interests of minority groups in the population. Even when there tends to be a consensus, for example, protecting the environment, there is no agreement about the cost or the speed of adopting policies to protect the environment. When there is a consensus about each of the two conflicting goals, governors have a choice between the horns of a dilemma: for example, whether to lock down the economy to protect popular health during the coronavirus pandemic or to allow economic and social activities to continue in order to protect people from unemployment, loss of income and social isolation.

Government of the people is achieved by placing it in the hands of politicians who are their elected representatives. The adversary division of the House of Commons into government and Opposition parties creates an obstacle to populist leaders claiming to represent the views of all the people. An essential feature of democracy is that representatives are elected by universal suffrage rather than by an electorate restricted to the well born, the well-off or a single ethnic or racial group. In Britain the people who govern are MPs representing millions but less than a majority of voters. Many voters do not want to be represented by people like themselves, but by people who have more understanding of government than they do (Hibbing and Theiss-Morse 2002).

Insofar as MPs are representative of the people who elect them, they combine public interest and self-interest in a variety of ways that make them more or less trustworthy. British democracy is healthy to the extent that its institutions are strong enough to curb passions of self-interest damaging to the interests of the people they represent.

1.2   ANATOMIZING THE BODY POLITIC

Democracy without government remains an abstraction. For the idea of democracy to have an impact on how a country is governed, it must be embodied in political institutions that form the anatomy of the body politic. Because the United Kingdom is a unitary state in which authority is centralized in Westminster, it can appropriately be described as a single political body. By contrast, the separation of powers and the American federal system create three political bodies in Washington, the Presidency, Congress and the Supreme Court, and more in its 50 states.

The heart of the body politic is the electoral system. Undemocratic as well as democratic systems pay tribute to the importance of elections in mobilizing a show of support for their authority. Thus, totalitarian political systems such as the Soviet Union made turning out to vote for the Communist Party compulsory, even though the result was a foregone conclusion.

A healthy democracy requires free and fair elections. Donald Trump's denunciation of the American electoral system as fraudulent illustrates the importance for democratic politics of the losing party conceding defeat without questioning the integrity of elections.

A distinctively British sign of good health is that the first-past-the-post electoral system makes a single party accountable for government by manufacturing a parliamentary majority for the party that wins a plurality of votes. This electoral system contrasts with the continental European version of a healthy system: it gives proportional representation to parties in parliament in keeping with their share of the popular vote. This has the side effect of resulting in coalition governments lacking the clarity of accountability of the British electoral system.

Parties connect the heart of the electorate with the brains of government through the veins of parliament. Parties decide who represents voters and may become a Cabinet minister because they control the process of nominating candidates. In an undemocratic political system, the central committee of the governing party decides who is nominated, and nomination is tantamount to election. In Britain candidates are not selected by a central committee at party headquarters; the choice is decentralized to more than 600 constituency parties that each nominate one candidate for Parliament. The process of nomination is democratically healthy if a party's MPs collectively represent the diversity of political views and social characteristics of its voters.

The need to give voters a clear choice of government means that MPs are not expected to give priority to representing the voters in their particular constituency, as is the case for Members of Congress in the United States. Instead, party democracy is in good health if in House of Commons divisions MPs vote as instructed by their parliamentary whips in support of the national programme on which they are elected. Voters can then decide at the next election whether to reaffirm their choice of governing party by voting for or against their constituency MP.

As the head of the body politic, the prime minister has overall responsibility for giving direction to government. The exercise of the prime minister's brainpower is restricted not only by his or her mental capacity; it is also bounded by the clock and the calendar. There are not enough hours in the week for a single politician to keep track of all the activities of government that he or she is nominally responsible for. Many of the prime minister's policy decisions are not their personal initiative but meta-decisions involving conflicting pressures. During the coronavirus pandemic the prime minister has had to decide between imposing major restrictions on contacts between people to reduce risks to life or to relax restrictions on contacts to avoid damage to the economy and social life.

A healthy democracy requires a prime minister who can do at least two jobs at once: maintain the support of the electorate and give direction to the government. It is a symptom of ill health if parties choose as their leader a politician who has never held government office before and must learn on the job in Downing Street how Whitehall works. It can be fatal to the governing party's hold on Downing Street if their leader does not maintain the confidence of voters. The Conservative party has been brutal in responding to symptoms that their leader is an election loser by ejecting him or her from Downing Street. Even though Margaret Thatcher had led the party to three successive election victories, in 1990 Conservative MPs forced her out of Downing Street when she appeared to threaten election defeat.

To treat the head of the body politic as the only political brain in government is misleading. Cabinet ministers and their departments are the backbone of government. For example, the minister at the Department of Transport is responsible for policies for airlines, roads, ships and railways; 24 non-departmental agencies are concerned with activities such as issuing licences to motorists and preventing rail accidents. The secretary of state for Transport is supported by five junior ministers.

Ministers supply the political muscle that is needed to wrestle with business interests, unions and not-for-profit organizations whose activities are affected by their department's policies. Ministers also use muscle to wrestle extra money from the Treasury and parliamentary time for presenting bills for approval by the House of Commons. A minister needs stamina to run the Whitehall obstacle race in which other departments are the hurdles. Fleet footwork is also needed to dodge questions from MPs and the media about departmental mistakes.

In order to give democratic direction to a department with dozens of responsibilities, thousands of staff and a budget of billions, ministers need management skills. Most MPs come to Whitehall experienced in managing their political career but never having managed a large organization. Nor are they accustomed to being surrounded by civil servants who advise on how or whether their ideas can be carried out. It is a sign of good health if a newly appointed minister has already served in government and if they stay in the same department long enough to become familiar with its activities and complete policies they have announced. Keeping a department in good health is a co-operative effort. It is a sign of ill health if there is friction between a minister's political advisers and civil servants in defining departmental policies and if a minister subject to criticism shifts blame on their civil servants.

The limbs of the body politic are not limited by nature as is the case with the human body. Westminster has spawned hundreds of progeny, public bodies that are authorized by an Act of Parliament and wholly or partly financed by the Treasury. Local governments are democratic because they are headed by elected councils, although most have an electorate only a little larger than a single parliamentary constituency. They are responsible for delivering major public services such as education, social care and refuse collection. However, the stature of local government is stunted because their powers are determined by Acts of Parliament. From Westminster's perspective, local government is in good health when it delivers satisfactory policies with the powers and money that Westminster allocates it. When the government is dissatisfied, it can take away responsibility for a policy. For example, Tony Blair's Labour government introduced academy schools to take bog-standard comprehensive schools out of the hands of local councils, many of which were Labour-controlled. From the perspective of English local government, health is bad when Westminster won't recognize that demands for services are rising faster than the amount of money that the Treasury provides to meet needs.

Devolved governments in Scotland, Wales and Northern Ireland not only have electoral legitimacy but also a claim to speak for the Scottish, Welsh or Irish people. Acts of the Westminster Parliament devolve more policies to these governments than are given to English local government. The heads of devolved governments would like to be treated as partners of the British prime minister in what they see as a Federal Kingdom. However, Whitehall views them as subordinate bodies best kept at a distance. Nationalist parties have a different definition of a healthy relationship: they want to be independent of the British government.

Electoral legitimacy is not the only source of political authority; many non-governmental agencies deliver public services on the grounds that they have the expertise to do so or that they can deliver public services more efficiently (cf. Dahl 1970; www.gov.uk/government/org anisations). The National Health Service consists of hospitals run by professional health administrators and surgeries run by doctors. There are also hundreds of quangos (quasi-autonomous government bodies) that carry out public policies at arm's length from ministries. Public management theories endorse contracting out public services to private sector firms that are assumed to be more efficient and cheaper than elected bodies. This approach appealed to Margaret Thatcher's 'business is better' philosophy, and the Labour government that followed her maintained contracting out.

Freedom from direct accountability to the electorate makes many of these agencies claim to be non-political rather than part of the body politic. Nonetheless, they derive their authority from Acts of Parliament and spend public money controlled by the Treasury. In the vague phrasing of a government website, they 'work with' a Whitehall department. Delegating public services to non-elected public bodies is healthy as long as the conditions that Whitehall sets are practicable, the money it provides is sufficient to meet costs and non-governmental agencies understand that their performance is subject to scrutiny by elected politicians. It is a symptom of poor health when an organization providing a public service fails to meet standards, for example, there is a riot in or an escape from a private prison. It is also a symptom of poor health when a Whitehall department's lack of capacity to contract out elaborate computer systems results in cost overruns of tens of millions of pounds or total failure.

The rule of law is the superego of the democratic body politic, imposing ethical norms as a constraint on the impulsive desires of the id and the realistic calculations of the ego. In this way, the separation of institutions produces a balance of powers. Courts give institutional force to the rule of law, making judgements that restrain impulses of government ministers to act beyond their powers. Traditionally, the British government has invoked the doctrine of the High Court of Parliament to justify being free of judicial constraint. In a democratic era, the government of the day, whether Conservative or Labour, invokes the legitimacy of popular election to justify being free of constraint by non-elected judges. British judges have tended to respond by keeping silent because an unwritten constitution leaves them without a document they can cite to justify their decisions and open to government accusations of interfering in politics if they declare a government action unconstitutional.

Given the vagueness inherent in an unwritten constitution, the relationship between the government of the day and the courts is healthiest when no political dispute arises about the constitutionality of government action. Such disputes are infrequent, because ministers and, even more, their civil service advisers have internalized norms about what government can and cannot do. It is a sign of political ill health when disputes arise about whether or not the government is acting within its powers in dealing with an issue of constitutional significance and there is no consensus about how to resolve the dispute in the absence of a constitutional court.

International relations tests the mental health of British ministers because the sense of being in control that comes with being nationally powerful is challenged by confronting self-confident foreign politicians who put looking after their own body politic ahead of satisfying British voters. When switching from domestic politics to international relations, British ministers need to think differently. Instead of relying on the party's whips to deliver approval for whatever the government decides, ministers must understand the interests and practices of other governments with whom they deal.

It is a sign of good mental health when British ministers approach international relations by looking at the weight of other countries and intergovernmental institutions before deciding how to promote British interests abroad. If the forces are heavyweights, then the British government can seek to form coalitions of mutual interest with other governments. It is a sign of bad mental health if the government seeks to punch above its weight and in consequence is flattened.

A clinical diagnosis is a hands-on examination of the body politic that checks whether democratic institutions work in practice as they are supposed to work in theory. Systematically examining the different parts of the body politic avoids generalizing about the health of the whole body from a single part; it shows which parts are working well and which parts aren't. Evaluating British democracy by comparison with a clinical model avoids relying on partisan standards defining good health as one's own party being the government of the day.

1.3 MANY SYMPTOMS OF ILL HEALTH

During the past quarter-century British political institutions and processes have shown a variety of symptoms departing from standards of perfect democratic health. They include:

- *The electoral system is unreliable in creating single-party government.* The British first-past-the-post electoral system offers voters a democratic choice of who governs, but it is a minimum choice. As long as the Conservative and Labour parties together command the support of the great majority of voters, the system fixes responsibility for the government on a single party. However, in the seven elections since 1997 up to a third of voters have shown they do not want either a Conservative or a Labour government. Moreover, in two of the past four elections, the electoral system failed to convert the winning party's plurality of votes into a parliamentary majority.
- *The demands of a political career set MPs apart from most voters.* To succeed in British politics today it is advisable to start young as an undergraduate active in a student Labour or Conservative club. However, a majority of Britons have not gone to university and working-class voters with less education are less likely to participate in politics. On graduating, aspiring politicians gravitate towards jobs that set them apart from most graduates; instead of going to work in the private sector they seek jobs that advance a political career— working for an MP, a think tank or in the media. If they win a seat in Parliament, they are set apart from most middle-class graduates.
- *A prime minister lacks the confidence of voters.* Neither Gordon Brown nor Theresa May ever won a general election, and David Cameron won a majority in only one of the three elections that he fought. Tony Blair was unusual in twice winning re-election.

However, in 2005, Blair's winning share of the vote was less than that of the losing candidate in every American presidential election since 1928. Boris Johnson's victory in the 2019 general election was not a popular endorsement of him personally; he benefited from voters giving Jeremy Corbyn a much bigger negative rating than he received.

- *Campaigning is now more important than governing.* A prime minister must be a good campaigner but this is only half the job; the other half is being in charge of the British government. Until Tony Blair became prime minister, tenants of Number 10 had first spent a decade or longer as ministers learning what government is about. Blair and David Cameron parachuted into Whitehall; the first government job each had was that of prime minister. During Boris Johnson's brief exposure to Whitehall as Foreign secretary he concentrated on campaigning to become prime minister rather than learning about the difficulties of turning campaign slogans into Acts of Parliament.

- *Winning an election can make ministers overconfident in the power of their will.* Blair entered Downing Street believing that because New Labour had won a smashing election victory he could easily make government new. May reacted negatively to learning that the slogan that gained her the prime ministership, 'Brexit means Brexit', was not practical politics when negotiating with the European Union. Downing Street spread the word that the problem of delivering Brexit was not her fault but that of the government's Permanent Representative to the EU, Ivan Rogers. He resigned and put on record unpleasant truths that May had tried to ignore (see Rogers 2019). Johnson was confident that he could spin a Brexit deal with Brussels as readily as he spun his way into Downing Street.

- *Policymaking is frequently disrupted by reshuffling ministers and reorganizing Whitehall departments.* For ministers new to a department, getting to grips with their responsibilities can take up to two years and turning manifesto commitments into Acts of Parliament can take most of a Parliament. The readiness of prime ministers to reshuffle ministers means that a significant number of ministers do not last two years in the same Whitehall department. Between 2015 and 2020 the Conservative government had three prime ministers, four Foreign secretaries, four Home secretaries and three Chancellors of the Exchequer. Prime ministers can also respond to chronic difficulties in achieving political goals by reorganizing Whitehall departments but this does not alter unsatisfactory policies.

- *High-ranking politicians behave shamefully when caught engaging in dubious political practices.* Britons do not expect their politicians to be plaster saints, but there is a belief that if politicians are caught behaving shamefully they should pay a political price (Rose and Wessels 2019). Although Peter Mandelson, the strategist of Labour's 1997 election victory, was twice caught giving misleading accounts about dealings with fellow Cabinet ministers, both Blair and Gordon Brown re-appointed Mandelson to high office after he spent a period out of office. When Johnson's chief strategist Dominic Cummings was found to have disregarded government rules against travelling during the coronavirus lockdown, Cummings' explanation was dismissed by public opinion, but Johnson, himself no stranger to romancing facts, accepted it.
- *Parties are in conflict about the boundaries of the United Kingdom.* In Northern Ireland a large minority wants unity with the Republic of Ireland, and the Irish Republican Army has intermittently sought to achieve the unification of Ireland by armed force. The UK government accepts Northern Ireland leaving the United Kingdom if a majority in a referendum votes for unification with the Irish Republic. UK policy on Scottish independence is at a stalemate. In 2014 the government approved a Scottish referendum on independence and pledged to accept the result, and the Scottish National Party (SNP) government accepted it was a once-in-a-generation vote. A majority in Scotland voted to remain in the Union. Since a majority of Scottish voters endorsed staying in the European Union in the 2016 Brexit referendum, the SNP government argues this has created a new situation justifying a second independence referendum. The Scottish Parliament has voted to hold such a ballot while the UK government has refused to authorize it.
- *Politicians and judges disagree about what an unwritten constitution allows governors to do.* Britain is an abnormal democracy because it lacks a written constitution, and the government of the day claims the right to act free of judicial constraint. Unusually, the UK Supreme Court did overrule Boris Johnson's advice to the Queen to prorogue Parliament during the Brexit process in 2019 and Johnson very grudgingly complied with the ruling. After winning a general election with a manifesto pledge to keep courts from interfering

in political decisions of government, Johnson has commissioned a review to recommend ways to enable the government to make decisions for which it claims an electoral mandate but which law professors could describe as unconstitutional.

- *Politicians look for a global role with an out-of-date map.* The limits on the power of the British government to act are both mental and physical. Britain's position as one of the world's three great powers at the end of the Second World War has left a legacy that encourages prime ministers to have high ambitions about Britain's place in the world. However, taking back control of significant policies from Brussels does not turn the calendar back to 1945. Today's global vision of Britain punching above its weight invites a knockout blow from heavyweight powers such as the United States and China. The Brexiters' belief in unqualified sovereignty is a delusion, a foreign policy without foreigners.

1.4   POTENTIALLY FATAL SYMPTOMS

The symptoms of ill health described above are like diabetes; they are chronic or intermittent conditions that if properly managed are not fatal. The death of democracy is the culmination of a process in which one or more vital organs of the body politic functions in an undemocratic way. Life-threatening symptoms of democratic ill health are a cancerous growth that requires surgery. If they are neglected, the result can be the death of a country's democracy.

Examining an established democracy may produce a bill of health free of any fatal symptoms. However, the motto 'Never say never in politics' is an apt warning against excessive confidence. The belief that it (that is, violent threats to democracy) can't happen here was shattered in the United States when President Donald Trump incited an armed crowd of supporters to storm Congress on 6 January 2021 to prevent it formally certifying his election defeat. The security measures at the Palace of Westminster today are a reminder that a Conservative MP, Airey Neave, was killed within its precincts by an Irish Republican car bomb in 1979.

Actions threatening representative institutions that can lead to the death of democracy include:

- Introducing political control of the media to prevent criticism of the government of the day.
- Arresting opposition politicians and disqualifying opposition political parties from contesting elections.
- Changing the rules of the electoral system to remove the possibility of the government being defeated.
- Using referendum institutions to hold a plebiscite, that is, a vote on an issue that predictably produces an overwhelming victory for the government.

Actions undermining political accountability that can lead to the death of democracy include:

- Giving cronies and party apparatchiks the power to make policy.
- Denying or whitewashing political mistakes.
- Ignoring constitutional constraints and flouting court orders.
- Packing the courts to neuter judicial constraint.
- Organizing violence and terrorism.

Most of the above conditions can be found in the Russian Federation since Vladimir Putin became president in 1998. Fatal symptoms of democracy occur in democracies too. During his four years in office President Donald Trump so challenged standards of a healthy democracy that he was twice impeached by Congress. Some European Union states are ineffective or even corrupt democracies and Hungary and Poland have gone further. The EU has formally placed each on a watch list because the Hungarian and Polish governments have been adopting measures that could be fatal to democracy.

While the British body politic is not in ideal shape, the unhealthy symptoms described in this chapter are not fatal. If they were, then British democracy would already be dead or in its death throes. It is not. By definition, intermittent symptoms of democratic ills can be remedied by measures that get rid of the causes of ill health. For example, if no party wins an overall majority at a general election, another general election can return the system to normal good health. If a condition is chronic, such as the gross under-representation of Liberal Democrat voters in Parliament, the fact that it has persisted for a century shows that it is not fatal.

REFERENCES

Centre for the Future of Democracy. 2020. *Global Satisfaction with Democracy*. Cambridge: Bennett Institute for Public Policy.

Collier, David, and Steven Levitsky. 1997. Democracy with Adjectives: Conceptual Innovation in Comparative Research. *World Politics* 49 (3): 430–451.

Dahl, Robert A. 1970. *After the Revolution? Authority in a Good Society*. New Haven: Yale University Press.

Etzioni, Amitai. 1985. Making Policy for Complex Systems: A Medical Model for Economics. *Journal of Policy Analysis and Management* 4 (1): 383–395.

Gagnon, Jean-Paul. 2018. 2,234 Adjectives: Descriptions of Democracy. *Democratic Theory* 5 (1): 92–113.

Hibbing, John, and E. Theiss-Morse. 2002. *Stealth Democracy*. New York: Cambridge University Press.

Kaase, Max, and Kenneth Newton. 1996. *Beliefs in Government*. Oxford: Oxford University Press.

Likierman, Andrew. 2020. The Elements of Good Judgment. *Harvard Business Review*, January/February.

Rogers, Sir Ivan. 2019. *9 Lessons in Brexit*. London: Short Books.

Rose, Richard, and Bernhard Wessels. 2019. Money, Sex and Broken Promises: Politicians' Bad Behaviour Encourages Distrust. *Parliamentary Affairs* 72 (3): 481–500.

Rose, Richard, and B. Guy Peters. 1978. *Can Government Go Bankrupt?* New York: Basic Books.

Wolinetz, Stephen, and Andrej Zaslove. 2018. *Absorbing the Blow: Populist Parties and Their Impact on Parties and Party Systems*. London: ECPR Press Rowman & Littlefield.

CHAPTER 2

Elections the Heart of Government

For an electoral system to be democratic it should offer the electorate a direct choice between parties competing to take control of government and periodic elections giving the electorate the opportunity to hold the government of the day accountable by re-electing it or ejecting it from office. The first-past-the-post (FPTP) electoral system decides constituency results by a winner-take-all procedure. The winner in each constituency is the candidate who secures the most votes cast, whether it is a plurality of votes or an absolute majority. By contrast, the great majority of European democracies offer voters the choice of a multiplicity of parties, and seats are allocated to a variety of parties by a system of proportional representation.

The justification for the British electoral system is that it not only offers a choice of parties but also offers a clear choice of government. It normally does this by manufacturing an absolute parliamentary majority for the party winning a plurality even if not a majority of the popular vote. Giving control of government to a single party enables voters to hold it accountable on the basis of what it does during its term of office. The following election offers voters the choice of re-electing the government of the day or of withdrawing their support and voting to replace it. The FPTP system in Britain also favours the identification of a single Opposition party; it is recognized as the shadow government, complete with a

© The Author(s), under exclusive license to Springer Nature Switzerland AG 2021
R. Rose, *How Sick Is British Democracy?*
Challenges to Democracy in the 21st Century,
https://doi.org/10.1007/978-3-030-73123-6_2

shadow prime minister and Cabinet. Thus, when deciding who governs, voters can make a comparative evaluation of existing and alternative governments. The result has been the rotation of control of government between the Conservative and Labour parties for almost a century.

Most European democracies make a different trade-off than the British FPTP system: they use proportional representation (PR) to elect a wider range of parties to parliament. Both types of electoral systems meet a basic requirement for a democratic electoral system: they give voters a choice between competing parties. However, their consequences for the formation of party government are different (cf. Thomassen 2014). Because MPs in a PR system are awarded in proportion to a party's share of the vote even if it is 5 per cent or less, the party with the most votes invariably falls short of having a parliamentary majority. Forming a government can take months of bargaining between parties to agree a coalition government that compromises the manifesto commitments on which each was elected. In Germany, for example, the Christian Democrat and Socialist parties emphasize their differences in competing for votes but may afterwards form a grand coalition government. In addition, control of government can change hands if a new coalition government is formed during a parliament without voters being consulted. Voters dissatisfied with a coalition government can vote to turn it out of office, but if they succeed there is no certainty about what the alternative government will be.

Because a large portion of the vote is necessary to win control of government under the FPTP system, coalition formation takes place within the Conservative and Labour parties before an election. The drafting of the party's manifesto usually leads to policies favoured by the more left-wing or right-wing groups within the party being dropped because the electorate is not polarized between two ideological extremes. To win control of government a party must gain the support of a substantial number of voters who place themselves a little to the right- or left-of-centre on survey scales measuring left/right attitude. Proportional representation systems give extreme and even undemocratic parties seats in Parliament. Thus, the German PR system awarded the extremist Alternative for Germany (AfD) party a position as the leading Opposition party in the Bundestag after it won 12.6 per cent of the vote in 2017, whereas the United Kingdom Independence Party gained no seats when it won 12.6 per cent of the vote in the British general election of 2015.

The British electoral system is not the product of a democratic theory. It reflects the accumulation of institutions that go back to medieval times, such as using the first-past-the-post system to determine winners to represent a geographical constituency. Democratization occurred by gradually expanding the franchise in the nineteenth century until universal suffrage for men and women was achieved in 1918. The decisions were made by MPs elected on the traditional system of representing communities.

The heart of the British body politic, the electoral system, is in good democratic health as long as it meets three essential standards. In every constituency voters have a fair and free choice between parties competing for government; the electoral system fixes responsibility for government by converting one party's votes into an absolute majority in Parliament; and voters can hold the government of the day accountable and vote to return it to office or reject it in favour of an alternative government.

2.1   Institutionalizing Choice

There are many ways to conduct a democratic election that converts millions of votes into a choice of government. The methods for doing so differ in major features, such as whether voters elect a president or MPs, and in minor features, such as whether elections are held on a weekday or at the weekend. A comparative review of national electoral systems has 996 pages (Herron et al. 2018). Electoral institutions are in good health as long as the laws regulating candidates and the methods for counting the votes and determining the winner are clear and fairly enforced and losers consent to the result rather than claim fraud as President Donald Trump did in 2020.

It is easy for people living in the United Kingdom to qualify to vote in a general election. It is not necessary to be a British citizen; UK residents who are Irish citizens or citizens of any of 54 Commonwealth countries are eligible to vote too. Nor is it necessary to be fluent in English; electoral registration forms are available in more than two dozen different languages. Youths under 18 can register to vote as long as they will reach that age if an election is held in the year ahead. Local government officials are responsible for maintaining an up-to-date register. Every year they circulate each household asking whether any names should be added to the electoral register or whether residents have moved away. People who move or find their name is not on the register can qualify to vote until shortly before election day. The Electoral Commission has recommended that, in order to guard against fraud, everyone should be asked for an authorized photo-identification card when being given a ballot. The Conservative government is proposing legislation to require photo identification for voting at the next general election. Labour MPs oppose it on the grounds that between 5 and 10 per cent of UK residents do not have photo identification; research indicates that these people are twice as likely to vote Labour as Conservative (House of Commons 2019).

When Britons cast their votes in a general election, the choice is deceptively simple: only one office is at stake. The ballot offers a choice between several candidates for the position of Member of Parliament for one of the United Kingdom's 650 constituencies. Since it is the candidate's national party label that primarily influences voting behaviour, voters are making a choice not about a local representative but about which party they want to form the government. By contrast, in the US voters are confronted with a long ballot that can list candidates for offices ranging from the president to the local coroner. Moreover, national elections offer choices for both branches of government, the presidency and Congress, and the outcome is often a government divided between two competing parties.

Election laws make it easy for almost any eligible voter to stand as a candidate in any constituency; a candidate need not be a resident there. All that is required is a nomination paper signed by ten of the constituency's electorate and a £500 deposit that will be returned if the candidate secures 5 per cent or more of the constituency vote. By American standards contesting a parliamentary election is very cheap, because there are strictly enforced laws that limit how much a candidate can spend. It varies with the size of the constituency and averages about £14,000. There is no limit on how much parties can spend nationally, but the ban on television advertising and the shortness of the election campaign require a pittance compared to what is spent in an American presidential election.

In the 2019 general election, 3320 candidates contested seats under 108 different party labels or as independents. Some labels refer to national issues, others to local concerns, and they may be frivolous, such as the Church of the Militant Elvis Party. Politicians who launch new parties or stand as independents are mistaken in assuming that there are many dissatisfied voters waiting to flock to them. Of the 500 candidates of parties that won no seats in Parliament or stood as independents, only one in eight saved their deposit by taking the required 5 per cent of the vote.[1]

Because constituency boundaries take historical communities and geography into account, their electorates vary in size. Constituency electorates vary between 21,000 in the Western Isles of Scotland to 113,000 in the Isle of Wight. At the 2019 election the average constituency in Wales had an electorate of 57,992, while in Scotland it was 18 per cent larger and in England 29 per cent larger. There is a bill in Parliament to reduce to 5 per cent the inequality in the number of electors that MPs represent. Labour opposes this on the grounds that it will disrupt ties between MPs and communities. It will also lead to the loss of about ten Labour MPs, because Labour tends to win in constituencies with smaller electorates than Conservative seats.

Four parties offer voters a choice in almost every constituency in Britain. The Conservative, Labour and Liberal Democrat parties each contested more than 600 seats in 2019 and the Green Party fought 497 seats. In Scotland and Wales, nationalist parties fought every seat, and in Northern Ireland two Unionist and two Irish parties fought almost every constituency. Four parties—the Conservatives, Labour, Liberal Democrats and the Scottish National Party—each won more than one million votes. The Green Party won 865,000 votes but only 32 Green candidates saved their deposit.

Party manifestos offer voters a prospect of policies they will adopt if they win control of the government. While few voters read manifestos, their major pledges are widely publicized. Each manifesto balances broad consensual pledges such as making the country more prosperous with specific pledges to attract particular groups of voters, for example, pensioners, students or women. There is also a need to restrain popular but costly pledges that opponents can attack. For example, a Labour pledge to spend more on a social policy can be attacked by Conservatives as threatening a rise in the income tax and a Conservative pledge to cut taxes can be attacked by Labour as threatening the National Health Service. Pledges that cost little in money or political capital are usually delivered. During the election campaign, departmental civil servants draft policies based on manifesto pledges so that whichever party wins there

---

[1] All statistics cited for the 2019 UK general election come from House of Commons (2020a) and for earlier elections from House of Commons (2020b).

is something positive to offer their new minister as soon as he or she is appointed.

The rotation of Conservative and Labour parties in and out of government creates a record in office that voters can use when deciding which party they want to control government. Past achievements can be cited for or against a party. For example, the Labour party today claims to be the party of the National Health Service because it was introduced by a Labour government long before the great majority of voters were born. A party's record in office can provide a reason for voting against it. Labour was helped to victory in 1997 by the Conservative government losing its reputation for sound management of the economy five years earlier when it was forced to devalue the pound. The Labour government was defeated in 2010 when Gordon Brown's policy of making the economy boom went bust after the 2008 global slump hit the British economy.

British laws strictly regulate many activities of parties and candidates and heavily restrict the formation and spending of political action groups. Compliance is monitored by opponents, resulting in prosecutions for violations being rare. Broadcasters are required to give a balanced coverage of parties in keeping with their electoral importance. Since parties generate unfavourable as well as favourable stories, both sides make complaints about media coverage; independent assessments find that coverage is balanced. The press tends to be strongly partisan in a symbiotic reflection of the readership to which it appeals (Electoral Commission 2020).

Because votes are counted publicly on election night under the scrutiny of observers from all parties, this avoids allegations of fraud. Since the ballot is simple, offering a single choice for a single office, there is no need for electronic voting machines that give an opening to allegations of vote-rigging. Only one-quarter of 1 per cent of ballots are ruled out of order, because they are unmarked or votes are given to more than one candidate. If losing candidates believe that the count is incorrect, they can request a recount. The request is allowed if the official in charge considers the margin of victory so narrow that a slight change in the vote count could change the winner; this very rarely happens. If a losing candidate believes the winner violated campaign laws, the court can be petitioned to declare the result void. Instances of constituency malpractice are relatively few as are challenges to the result (cf. Fisher and Sällberg 2020).

The explosive expansion of digital technology has altered the methods by which political parties campaign and encouraged freelance interventions. Instead of engaging in face-to-face canvassing of voters as was the case a century ago, parties can now make virtual contact and, with databases documenting social characteristics of voters, appeal to their specific social interests. Digital technology can be used to disseminate political views in ways that are not transparent or subject to regulation by existing election laws. Cross-party groups are now seeking to develop measures that would allow free and robust social media campaigning within a legal framework requiring transparency and political accountability (House of Lords 2020).

2.2   Responsibility for Government Fixed

In order for voters to be sure whom to credit or blame for the performance of government, the electoral system should fix responsibility for the government on a single party by giving a disproportionately large number of seats to the party with the most votes. It thus avoids the consequence of proportional representation, which divides seats much more in accordance with their share of the vote, thereby producing coalition governments that involve compromises in the manifesto pledges of the parties participating in the coalition.

Because every constituency ballot offers a choice of up to half a dozen candidates, there is no need for the winner to secure an absolute majority of the vote; a plurality of votes is sufficient to win. The electoral system converts the leading party's plurality in the popular vote into an absolute majority in the House of Commons. No party has won an absolute majority of the popular vote since 1935 and in only three elections has it failed to give a single party an absolute majority in Parliament. In each case, the upshot was that at the following general election the governing party won an absolute majority of seats.

Because the total number of MPs that the governing party wins depends on the complicated addition of 650 different constituency results, the share of the vote needed to win a majority of seats varies from election to election. Boris Johnson gained control of the government in 2019 because the Conservative party gained a majority of 80 in the House of Commons with 43.6 per cent of the popular vote, whereas Theresa May lost the majority that David Cameron had won in 2015 in spite of winning 5.5 percentage points more of the vote than her predecessor. In

2005 Tony Blair won 355 seats and a third term in Downing Street, even though Labour's share of the vote was less than 1 per cent more than Neil Kinnock had gained in 1992, when it left Labour in opposition with only 271 seats.

The extremely unstable relationship between winning votes and seats has been demonstrated by the party coming second in the popular vote—the Conservatives in 1951 and Labour in February 1974—nevertheless winning the most MPs. The fluctuating nature of the share of the vote needed to win a parliamentary majority was demonstrated in the 2017 election. Even though the vote share of Theresa May's party was within 1 per cent of that giving Boris Johnson and Tony Blair their comfortable parliamentary majorities, the Conservatives won only a plurality of MPs and returned to Downing Street as head of a minority government supported by the Northern Ireland Democratic Unionist Party.

The party that finishes second nationally in votes usually has enough constituency strongholds so that the number of MPs it wins tends to approximate its share of the overall vote. In 2019 Labour won 32.1 per cent of the vote and 30.1 per cent of MPs, while in 2005, the last election the Conservatives lost, it took 31.0 per cent of MPs with 32.4 per cent of the vote. The ability of 'third' parties to win seats depends on whether their support is concentrated or evenly spread around the country. Thus, in 2019 the Scottish National Party's 3.9 per cent of the UK vote gave it almost twice that proportion of seats in Parliament because it amounted to 45.0 per cent of the vote in Scotland. The first-past-the-post system has impartially penalized both the Liberal Democrats and the United Kingdom Independence Party (UKIP) because their vote is widely spread. In 2015 UKIP gained 12.6 per cent of the national vote but only one seat, and in 2019 the Liberal Democrats' 11.5 per cent of the national vote gained it only 1.7 per cent of the seats in the House of Commons.

Every election gives voters the alternative of re-electing or ejecting the government of the day. If the governing party was always re-elected, that would be a symptom of political ill health, since in a democracy control of government ought to rotate. If the government party was always defeated, that too would be a symptom of sickness, implying that neither of the parties rotating in control of government was deemed fit to govern.

In 13 of the 20 elections since 1950, voters have expressed confidence in the government of the day by re-electing it, and since 1974 each Opposition party that has gained Downing Street has succeeded in winning re-election at least once. The Conservatives have won re-election three times after Margaret Thatcher's initial victory in 1979 and three times since David Cameron became prime minister in 2010. Tony Blair was twice re-elected after his 1997 landslide victory, and Labour governments have three times been re-elected once. Ted Heath is the only post-war prime minister who failed to win re-election at least once.

The government of the day more often wins re-election by gaining votes and seats, rather than by holding on to its majority even though it loses some seats. Once a leader moves from Opposition to the government, he or she becomes a very visible and authoritative national figure and not just a party leader who has never shown whether they were up to the challenge of government. Both Harold Wilson and Margaret Thatcher benefited from this effect, substantially boosting their parliamentary majority after demonstrating their mettle in office. Winning a landslide initial victory makes it more difficult for a party to see its vote go up further, but offers plenty of leeway for the government to lose votes and seats and still retain its grip on government. Blair's landslide victory in 1997 gave Labour a lead of 241 seats over its opponents. Thus, Labour could keep its absolute parliamentary majority even though it lost dozens of seats in the next two elections.

The government of the day is often helped in winning re-election by the party it defeats being slow to react to its loss of electoral appeal. After Labour's 1979 defeat, Michael Foot won the leadership on a left-wing platform and fought the next election with a manifesto that one of its MPs dubbed the longest suicide note in history. The Conservative government gained an additional 58 seats even though its vote dropped because the Labour party's vote drop of 9.3 percentage points was given to the Social Democrats and the Liberals. Labour needed to fight three more elections before it could recover. When the Conservative Party lost one-quarter of its vote in 1997, the Labour government benefited by its vote going up one-quarter.

The paradox of power is that the longer a party is in government, the closer it comes to leaving office. Longevity in office hands the Opposition party a simple slogan: 'It's time for a change'. Governors tend to forget that their election owes more to the attention they showed voters than to their own personality or their activities in Whitehall (see Chapter 3). After Thatcher won her third successive election victory, an official in Conservative Central Office told me that its priority was to run a campaign to politicize the Conservative government: that is, to make it aware of the need to win re-election. Thatcher then introduced the poll tax on housing without thinking about its effect on voters. The effect was fatal on her leadership; Conservative MPs who were worried about losing their seats ejected her from Downing Street.

After winning re-election in 2001, Tony Blair gave priority to his ambition of becoming a world leader by aligning himself with the United States in the Iraq War. The immediate consequence was a decline in his opinion poll ratings in Britain and the party losing 55 seats at the 2005 election. The longer-term consequence was that by 2017 an ORB poll for the *Independent* found that Blair was more unpopular with Labour voters than Jeremy Corbyn and that 72 per cent of the general public had an unfavourable opinion of Blair.

The British system produces a prompt choice of government too. Within 24 hours of the last vote being cast, the leader of the winning party receives the Queen's commission to form a government. There is no waiting for weeks, months or even a year for haggling about a coalition to end and a new government to be formed. Nor is there any 'switch-selling' of government during the life of a Parliament, as happens if one coalition breaks up and a new coalition government is formed without a fresh election giving it a popular mandate. In Italy there have been 19 elections and 61 governments since the end of the Second World War. This has produced an average of three governments for each parliament that Italians elect.

A unique British experience in coalition government occurred after the 2010 general election when the Conservative party won the most seats but lacked a parliamentary majority and the Liberal Democrats, with 57 MPs, were keen to become part of a peacetime government for the first time in almost a century. After discussions with both the Conservative and Labour leaders, the Liberal Democrats became partners in a coalition government in which David Cameron was the prime minister and the Liberal Democrat leader, Nick Clegg, became the deputy prime minister. Cameron welcomed the partnership as giving the Conservatives a more centrist image and restraining its right-wing MPs, while many Liberal Democrats were unhappy because they saw Labour as the party's natural ally. Voters rejected the coalition experiment at the 2015 general election. The Liberal Democrats lost more than seven-eighths of their MPs, and the Conservatives won an absolute parliamentary majority.

2.3 WHAT VOTERS MAKE OF THEIR CHOICE

At each general election the first choice that people must make is whether or not to vote. An individual voter cannot rationally hope to decide the outcome in their constituency, where tens of thousands of votes are needed to win, let alone be decisive in a national election. Although voting is not compulsory, most people see it as a civic duty, and they usually do their duty and vote. This is the case even when people know that the party they favour has no chance of winning in their constituency.

Turnout at general elections since 1997 has ranged between 71.4 per cent at the ballot that first returned Tony Blair's government, and 59.4 per cent when Blair was re-elected in 2001. In the 2019 election turnout was 67 per cent. The highest turnout on record, 83.9 per cent, was in the hard-fought and closely contested 1950 general election (House of Commons 2020b: 25). Turnout is artificially lowered because it is calculated by dividing the number of votes cast by the number of names on the electoral register, and electoral registration officers are slow to remove the names of voters when they die or move away from a constituency. It is also legal to register at two addresses, and students and people with second homes often do so. It is only illegal to vote twice. If the turnout at a general election ever came close to 100 per cent it would be evidence of massive fraud.

Most non-voters at a particular election are people who normally vote but occasionally miss out doing so; they are not politically alienated. The chief reasons for not voting at a particular election are non-political. On election day non-voters can be away from home on holiday or business; ill or forgetful; or put off by the weather. By the time people are middle-aged, the majority will have voted in most general elections in which they were eligible, and as they grow older the habit of voting increases at each election.

The first-past-the-post electoral system assumes that the great majority of voters are satisfied with having their choice of government reduced to the democratic minimum of two parties. From 1950 to 1970, this was the case, as the Conservative and Labour parties together won an average of 91.8 per cent of the UK vote. However, in the two elections held during the political and economic crisis of 1974, their combined support fell to 75 per cent. Subsequently, the two-party share of the vote has fluctuated. In three elections from 2005 to 2015 they averaged two-thirds of the

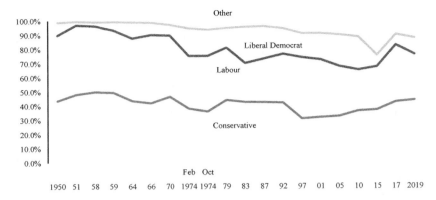

Fig. 2.1 Vote of Conservative, Labour and Liberal parties since 1950 (*Source* House of Commons Library 2020b: 12)

vote; the two-party share of the vote at the two most recent elections has been above 75 per cent (Fig. 2.1).

The main cause of the structural fall in the support for the two governing parties has been the Liberal Democrats transforming themselves from a party nominating candidates in a minority of seats to a party competing for votes nationwide. Between 1951 and 1970 the Liberals usually fought only one-third of all constituencies. Approximately two-thirds of the governing parties' fall in vote between 1970 and 1974 was due to the Liberal party almost doubling the number of its candidates. In elections from 1974 to the present, the Liberals have fought an average of more than 600 constituencies. The fresh appearance of a Liberal candidate in hundreds of constituencies enabled voters who had previously supported the Conservatives or Labour as a second choice to cast their ballot for their first choice, the Liberals, or Liberal Democrats as they were latterly renamed.

The volatility of the Conservative and Labour vote has increased as a consequence of the Liberal Democrats offering an alternative to voting for one of the two parties of government. Between the 1950 and 1970 elections the range between the highest and lowest vote for the Labour vote was 5.7 percentage points; it was 7.5 percentage points for the Conservatives. Since then the volatility of the Labour vote has more than doubled to 15.6 percentage points and that of the Conservative party to 13.2

points. Volatility no longer reflects a symmetrical swing in which the share of the vote that one party gains is matched by the other party's loss; the ups and downs of the Liberal Democrats impact both parties. In 2015 its electoral collapse enabled the vote for both the Conservative and Labour parties to rise notwithstanding their losses to UKIP. In 2017 the collapse of UKIP gave both the Conservative and Labour parties a big boost. In 2019 Labour lost one-fifth of its vote while the Conservatives gained barely 1 percentage point; the big gainers were a variety of third parties.

Voters have become open-minded in their choice of party at each election because of the decline of forces producing a lifelong commitment to a single party. The theme of the path-breaking study of *Political Change in Britain* was stability. Butler and Stokes (1969: 45) approvingly quoted the Gilbert and Sullivan verse that every child born alive was 'either a little Liberal or a little Conservative' to illustrate party loyalties being transmitted from one generation to the next. People who have a party identification do not need to choose between parties when an election is called; they reflexively vote for the party they identify with. In 1964 more than 90 per cent of respondents identified with a party, and the median group strongly identified with their party. The influence of class reinforced long-term party loyalty. A half-century ago almost two-thirds of middle-class voters favoured the Conservative party, while working-class voters favoured Labour by a margin of two to one (Gallup Poll 1976: 106f.).

By the 1980s more than one-third of the electorate did not know how their parents voted or, if they did know, their parents voted for different parties. Only two in five voted as their parents did, and the median group of voters described their party identification as not very strong. By 2019 party identification had weakened so much that a plurality did not identify with any political party, outnumbering those with a strong party identification by a margin of two to one (cf. Fieldhouse et al. 2020: 53). The Labour party is now a coalition of educated middle-class and traditional working-class voters (Evans and Tilley 2017). At the 2019 election the Conservatives won a plurality among both middle-class and working-class voters.

Today most Britons are floating voters; they have no party identification or only a weak and potentially transitory attachment to a party. They can make their choice of party government free of inherited loyalties. An increasing proportion of voters are floating voters, switching between parties from one election to the next. In 1966 only one in eight voted for a different party than they had endorsed two years before. By 2015 the proportion of switching their choice had risen to two-fifths (Fieldhouse et al. 2020: 13). Only a small fraction of the electorate is monogamous, voting for the same party at every election.

At the 2019 general election Boris Johnson took advantage of the increased fluidity of the electorate by appealing to traditional voters in the South of England and winning many seats in the North of England that had previously returned Labour MPs for up to three-quarters of a century. The Labour vote was also a disparate coalition; it consisted of traditional working-class voters, minority ethnic groups and educated middle-class voters who tended to agree more with each other and their MPs on economic policies than on issues of cultural identity.

When voters become dissatisfied with two alternative parties of government, they can vote for a third party. If a third party appears to be gaining support by adopting a fresh issue, such as protection of the environment, the governing parties can adopt pro-environment policies to protect their joint control of government. The Green movement's success as a pressure group has undermined its effort to become a major party in Parliament. Even though there is majority support for green policies to protect the environment, the Green Party's vote is minimal. At the 2019 election, it won only 2.7 per cent of the national vote and returned only one MP. The party's electoral failure is due to the electoral system offering pro-environment voters two choices. The first—Which party comes closest to your views?—favours the Green Party. However, the second—Do you want a Conservative or a Labour government?—offers a more important political choice.

Because marginal changes in votes can have a disproportionate effect on control of government, a fall in the vote for the governing parties can be a stimulus to good health as long as losers respond to such a signal of dissatisfaction. The weakening of party identification makes it easier for voters to signal their dissatisfaction with a party they have normally supported in the past. By-elections during the life of a Parliament offer an opportunity for supporters of the governing party to signal their dissatisfaction without risking their party losing office. Over the years both Conservative and Labour governments have usually responded sufficiently to signals of dissatisfaction to win re-election at least once. After a more or less prolonged period of internal disagreement about how to respond to defeat, the Opposition has regained enough popular support to eject the governing party from office and maintain the democratic requirement that control of government should rotate between parties.

In an electoral system designed to produce a choice, Britain's membership of the European Union created a symptom of ill health. As governors of an EU member state, Conservative and Labour ministers participated in EU policymaking; doing so enabled the British government to exert influence over a variety of EU policies, most notably the Single European Market, and to opt out of policies such as adopting the euro (Thomson 2011). Conservative and Labour leaders did not want to make EU membership an issue, because both parties had significant minorities which, for different reasons, opposed belonging to an institution that placed restrictions on the sovereignty of Parliament.

By contrast with the governing parties, the electorate has been divided about EU membership. When a referendum was held in 1975 about confirming the United Kingdom's entry, almost one-third voted against membership. In the decades that followed a significant minority and occasionally a plurality expressed opposition to the EU (Westlake 2020: 182–189). However, when anti-EU parties stood for Parliament and the choice was which party do you want to govern Britain, the result showed how strong was the barrier to their cause created by the first-past-the-post electoral system. Nigel Farage, the leader of the UKIP, fought seven elections as a candidate for UK Parliament and lost every time, usually finishing third or fourth.

When an election was not about which party governs Britain but about representing UK opinion in the European Parliament (EP), the change produced a different outcome for UKIP. The award of seats by proportional representation in EP elections also benefited smaller parties. In 1999 anti-EU candidates won four seats and Nigel Farage started his 20-year term as a Member of the European Parliament. At the 2014 election, UKIP won the most British seats in the European Parliament, thereby gaining substantial resources to campaign in domestic politics.

Since polls showed a substantially higher level of popular support for leaving the EU than for voting for an anti-EU party to govern Britain, Eurosceptics launched a campaign for a referendum on whether Britain should remain a member of the European Union. This call was supported by a number of backbench Conservative MPs. David Cameron conceded the demand, fearing that otherwise UKIP candidates would gain enough votes to prevent the Conservatives from winning a parliamentary majority at the 2015 general election. The calculations of both sides were rewarded. The Conservative government won a parliamentary majority and the anti-EU side gained a referendum that was held the following year.

The combination of an issue-cleavage that cut across party lines and the long-term decline in party identification temporarily created what two academics described as Brexitland, a realignment of voters according to their self-conscious identification with being for or against membership in the European Union (Sobolewska and Ford 2020: 11f.). The referendum ballot simply asked 'Should the United Kingdom remain a member of the European Union or should the United Kingdom leave the European Union?' Voters could not look to the party they identified with for guidance, since both the Conservative and Labour parties were divided on the issue. Thus, both the vote for leaving the EU and the vote for remaining consisted of cross-party coalitions of voters with a variety of different general election preferences. Since an absolute majority was required to win the referendum, the 51.9 per cent majority for Brexit (that is, leaving the EU) was higher than the vote for either governing party since the 1935 general election and the vote for leaving was higher than that for any governing party since the 1959 election. UKIP voters at the 2015 election contributed only one-quarter of the Leave vote.

The May 2019 election of British Members of the European Parliament became a second referendum on EU membership since the government of Britain was not at stake. The proportional representation system gave the newly created Brexit Party led by Nigel Farage two-fifths of the EP seats, and pro-EU parties collectively won almost as many. The two parties of government, the Conservatives and Labour, took barely one-quarter of the total vote and finished third and fifth respectively.

The general election in December 2019 demonstrated the resilience of the Conservative and Labour parties when the issue was which party should govern Britain and when MPs were allotted by the first-past-the-post electoral system. The Conservative party won votes from those giving priority to Brexit by emphasizing that it was the only party that could deliver Brexit by taking control of the government. The Brexit Party confirmed this by not nominating candidates in Conservative-held constituencies. The Conservative vote returned to the level of a governing party before Europe was an issue, and Labour achieved a second-place finish appropriate to the alternative government. The Liberal Democrats, unable to appear as a party of government, dropped from second in seats in the EP election to fifth place in the British Parliament (McAllister and Rose 2020: Table 5.1). Since the Labour Opposition under Keir Starmer has accepted Brexit as a given, Europe is no longer an issue in competition for control of party government. Simultaneously, the coronavirus pandemic has become the dominant issue and forced parties to compete on different grounds: which party is more likely to be effective in dealing with the deadly threat of coronavirus.

The first-past-the-post electoral system is normally in good health because it does what it is supposed to do: fixing responsibility for the government on a single party that voters can hold accountable at the next election. Critics are correct in describing it as a system of disproportional representation. However, distortion is a matter of degree, not kind. Proportionality in the November 2019 Spanish election was 85 per cent; in the 2019 FPTP election in the UK election it was 83 per cent. Converting the British system to proportional representation would increase the degree to which there was a match between the preferences of voters and the distribution of MPs, especially benefiting the Liberal Democrats and costing the Scottish National Party seats (cf. Table 6.1). However, it would have a cost, replacing elections in which voters decide who governs with a system in which post-election bargaining determines which parties form a coalition government and what its policies are.

British voters prefer the first-past-the-post electoral system. As a condition of supporting a Conservative government, the Liberal Democrats demanded a referendum on changing the electoral system, and a referendum in 2011 offered a choice between the existing system and the Alternative Vote system in which voters rank candidates in their order of preference. The second and third preferences of candidates at the bottom of the poll are redistributed until one of the leading candidates receives an absolute majority of votes. While the Alternative Vote is not a proportional representation system, it would give the Liberal Democrats more MPs and thereby make election outcomes more proportional. The popular choice was clear: 68 per cent endorsed keeping the first-past-the-post system. Because the turnout was only 42 per cent, only 13 per cent of the registered electorate endorsed a change in the electoral system.

References

Butler, David, and Donald Stokes. 1969. *Political Change in Britain*. London: Macmillan.

Electoral Commission. 2020. *UK Parliamentary General Election 2019*. London: The Electoral Commission.

Evans, Geoffrey, and James Tilley. 2017. *The New Politics of Class*. Oxford: Oxford University Press.

Fieldhouse, Edward, et al. 2020. *Electoral Shocks*. Oxford: Oxford University Press.

Fisher, Justin, and Yohanna Sällberg. 2020. Electoral Integrity. *British Journal of Politics and International Relations* 22 (3): 404–420.

Gallup Poll. 1976. Voting Behaviour in Britain, 1945–1974. In *Studies in British Politics*, ed. R. Rose, rev. ed., 204–215. London: Macmillan.

Herron, Erik S., R.J. Pekkanen, and M.S. Shugart (eds.). 2018. *The Oxford Handbook of Electoral Systems*. Oxford: Oxford University Press.

House of Commons. 2019. *Voter ID: Key Facts and Figures*. London: House of Commons Library Insight, Published 23 October.

House of Commons. 2020a. *General Election 2019: Results and Analysis*, 2nd ed. London: House of Commons Library Briefing Paper CBP 8749.

House of Commons. 2020b. *UK Election Statistics: 1918–2019*. London: House of Commons Library Briefing Paper CBP 7529.

House of Lords. 2020. *Digital Technology and the Resurrection of Trust*. London: House of Lords Select Committee on Democracy and Digital Technologies, Paper 77.

McAllister, Ian, and Richard Rose. 2020. When Institutions and Issues Change, Voting Changes. In R. Rose, *How Referendums Challenge European Democracy: Brexit and Beyond*, 77–99. London: Palgrave.

Sobolewska, Maria, and Robert Ford. 2020. *Brexitland*. Cambridge: Cambridge University Press.

Thomassen, Jacques. 2014. *Elections and Democracy: Representation and Accountability*. Oxford: Oxford University Press.

Thomson, Robert. 2011. *Resolving Controversy in the European Union*. Cambridge: Cambridge University Press.

Westlake, Martin. 2020. *Slipping Loose: The UK's Long Drift Away from the European Union*. Newcastle upon Tyne: Agenda.

CHAPTER 3

Party as the Lifeblood of Government

When Parliament gained power over the monarchy it created a parliamentary government. Democratization changed that: parliamentary government became party government. The government of the day is controlled by the party that has the most seats in the House of Commons. The choice of MPs is no longer in the hands of an oligarchy; it is determined by the votes of a mass electorate. As soon as the outcome of a general election is known, the Queen asks the leader of the party that wins a parliamentary majority to form a government. Democracy has replaced the government's accountability to independent-minded MPs who could literally own their constituency with accountability to an electorate that periodically has the option of re-electing or ejecting the government of the day.

MPs in the governing party are immediately accountable to their party whips, who herd their MPs into the division lobby to endorse government legislation. In the words of a Labour Cabinet minister, 'It's carrying democracy too far if you don't know the result of the vote beforehand' (quoted in Rose 1989: 121). It is the party label of MPs, not their personality, that is most important for their re-election. An aspiring politician cannot hope to win a seat in Parliament by standing as an independent. He or she must be selected to fight either a safe seat that their party has held for decades or a marginal seat that can be won by a national swing to

R. Rose, *How Sick Is British Democracy?*
Challenges to Democracy in the 21st Century,
https://doi.org/10.1007/978-3-030-73123-6_3

the party. The hundreds of MPs who win their seat with a plurality do not represent a majority of their constituency's voters, and each is only one among 650 MPs in the House of Commons. Clement Attlee was fond of quoting a Labour MP's explanation of why he voted as the party's whips instructed: 'When I was young I used to talk a lot about voting my conscience. I now see it was just my blooming conceit'.

In addition to representing a party and a geographical constituency, MPs with different social backgrounds bring to Parliament a variety of experiences of life. In keeping with the growing diversity of the electorate, parties now encourage the selection of candidates from all kinds of backgrounds. This has resulted in a great increase in the number of MPs who are women or from Black, Asian and minority ethnic backgrounds. MPs may draw on personal experience when relevant to an issue, such as sexual harassment, or on constituency issues if they represent an agricultural area or a place with high unemployment. However, when a vote is called in the House of Commons, MPs divide along party lines.

As long as MPs support their party in votes in the House of Commons, they are free to represent values, causes and interests that they think important. Their views may reflect divisions between parties such as how the tax burden should be distributed; divisions within parties such as Labour views on Palestine or Conservative views on same-sex marriage; or policies that tend to unite MPs across party lines such as the protection of the environment.

The next sections evaluate the health of British democracy by examining the way in which parties decide who they nominate in constituencies that they expect to win, and the extent to which this results in the presence in Parliament of MPs representing the social diversity of Britain today. It is followed by presenting empirical evidence of the political views of MPs on economic and social issues and comparing them with the views of their party's voters. The chapter concludes by showing that while MPs may influence public policy, they cannot act as a policymaking government.

3.1   Parties Decide Who Can Be an MP

To become an MP, an aspiring politician shops nationwide for a parliamentary nomination, since there is no requirement for residence in the constituency prior to being nominated. The ideal is to be selected to succeed an MP retiring in a safe seat where nomination is tantamount to election. On average, 86 incumbent MPs stand down at a general election after having served 18 years in the Commons and won election at least four times.

The second-best alternative is to be nominated to fight a marginal seat held by the party's opponents. The number of marginal seats that the Opposition party seeks to win depends on the political situation. After the 2019 election, there were 141 seats won by a margin of 10 percentage points and divided among eight different parties. To form a government after the next general election, Labour candidates would need to win all the marginal seats that the Conservatives now hold. On election day a candidate's efforts to win a marginal seat have little effect on the outcome. It is the party's brand label that delivers the vote that a candidate needs to enter Parliament. No MP has been elected independent of a political party since the 2005 election.

Constituency parties normally choose the candidate who is the local standard-bearer of the national party, while their national party sets rules for approving candidates. In seats with an incumbent MP, the incumbent is normally re-nominated without opposition. In marginal seats and in by-elections, the national party headquarters promotes individuals who are expected to have the best chance of winning. Where the party's cause is hopeless and the constituency party may be virtually moribund, it can turn to the national organization to help it find someone who would be willing to be its nominee, often a young person wanting to gain the experience of campaigning before moving to fight a winnable seat.

In order to weed out political chancers and people with marks against their personal reputation, the Conservative party limits a constituency's choice to individuals who have first passed an all-day examination conducted by its Parliamentary Assessment Board. In constituencies in which an incumbent Conservative MP is retiring or which the party is targeting as winnable, party headquarters, after consulting local association officers, fixes a shortlist of three candidates from which constituency party members make a choice.

Instead of maintaining a list of individuals approved as candidates, the Labour party selection procedure endorses categories of individuals that constituency parties should consider as candidates 'in order to reflect the full diversity of society in terms of gender, race, sexual orientation and disability and to increase working-class representation' (Criddle 2016: 341). The Labour government's 2010 Equalities Act included an explicit provision to allow parties to have all-women shortlists to increase the proportion of women among Labour MPs. The party's Rule Book sets out procedures for the National Executive Committee to suspend its normal procedures 'when the NEC are of the opinion that the interests of the party would be best served by the suspension of the procedures issued by the NEC'. Tony Blair's patronage secured safe North of England seats for his London-born and Oxford-educated special advisers such as Peter Mandelson and the Miliband brothers. They quickly became MPs and ministers in Blair's government. Jeremy Corbyn's election was promoted by a left-wing activist movement that intimidated Blairite MPs by threatening to de-select them if they did not follow a left-wing line.

There are two ways in which aspiring politicians can enter Parliament: they can be the party's candidate to succeed an incumbent MP in a safe seat or win a marginal seat. Replacing an incumbent MP is the easier route. Since more than five-sixths of seats do not change hands between parties at a general election, the chances of gaining a marginal seat depend on whether the national swing is to the candidate's party or to the opponents. A massive turnover of MPs occurred as part of the Labour landslide victory in 1997; 37 per cent of constituencies returned new MPs. By contrast, the snap 2017 election in which few seats changed hands resulted in 551 incumbent MPs being re-elected. At the 2019 general election, a total of 155 seats returned new MPs. In 81 seats this was due to a different party winning the seat and in 74 constituencies the winning party did not change when the incumbent retired, usually on the grounds of age.

Fragmenting the power to nominate candidates among more than 600 constituency parties is politically healthy because it encourages MPs to be chosen for diverse reasons by hundreds of different constituency associations rather than by the party headquarters or party leader packing Parliament with their handpicked candidates. In effect, the process for choosing MPs is a market. In the absence of candidates being required to live in a constituency to become its candidate, ambitious politicians can scan the political map seeking a constituency that suits their personal taste as well as offering a good chance to become an MP. Constituency association members can interview aspiring candidates differing in their politics, personality and socio-economic characteristics. The vote of constituency party members is subject to multiple influences. The outcome is sometimes a surprise, to the chagrin of the front-runner and the surprise of the nominee.

Contrary to generalizations that every constituency association is either dominated by Tories who reject the twenty-first century or those who see the two-party system as divided into Trotskyites and Marxists, their members are not extremists. The average party member tends to hold views similar to those of party voters and MPs, while on economic issues a significant minority of Conservative party members hold centrist views, and on social issues a significant minority of Labour members hold conservative rather than liberal views (cf. Bale et al. 2020).

3.2   REPRESENTING SOCIETY IN PARLIAMENT

Since the introduction of democratic suffrage, Britons have cast their votes for the party that they identify as best representing their political values and interests. In their role as voters, individuals give priority to party identification rather than to their identity with their community or its football team. Political parties have sought support from all sections of society. The 1918 constitution of the Labour party described it as representing workers by hand or brain and since the time of Benjamin Disraeli the Conservative party has claimed, with varying degrees of empirical justification, to represent one nation. Both parties today draw a significant portion of their votes from citizens with diverse social characteristics. The relevance of class identities has so declined that the Conservatives no longer win the support of half the middle class and Labour no longer wins the vote of as much as half the working class (House of Commons 2020a: 53ff.).

Theories of the politics of presence add a second condition to democratic representation: Members of Parliament should represent not only political values but also the diversity of a society that is differentiated along gender, racial, ethnic and other lines (Phillips 1995). Social diversity should ensure that when issues are discussed in Parliament there will be MPs present who can contribute by drawing on their first-hand knowledge of such things as racial abuse, sexual harassment or needing government income assistance grants. This does not mean the division of voters into separate constituencies based on such identities as race, which was done in apartheid South Africa. In Britain the social diversity of the House of Commons depends on the choices that political parties make in the nomination of candidates.

When Margaret Thatcher became Britain's and Europe's first woman prime minister in 1979, almost 98 per cent of Conservative MPs and 96 per cent of Labour MPs were White males. She was the only woman in her Cabinet. Social and cultural change since has altered the face of British society. The BBC news is no longer presented just by White men speaking with a distinctive BBC accent. Women and men of varied races and sexual orientations are now familiar faces on television.

In a society in which White English heterosexual males are less than two-fifths of the electorate, political parties have accepted the principle that their MPs should represent a diverse mixture of people. This was formally confirmed in the all-party Speaker's Conference on Parliamentary Representation. It recommended that parties should rectify 'the disparity between the representation of women, ethnic minorities and disabled people in the House of Commons and their representation in the population at large' (House of Commons 2010: 340). It suggested a large number of measures to encourage a more socially diverse Parliament. No numerical quota was recommended. It left to each party the choice of measures to adopt in keeping with the socio-economic composition of the people they represent. Both party headquarters have actively taken steps to promote the nomination of candidates from social groups under-represented in the Commons.

Consistent with a slim majority of the electorate being women, nominating more women candidates in winnable seats has been the first priority of parties. In the 2019 election 220 women were elected as Members of Parliament, a record total and an increase of more than three-quarters since the Speaker's Conference Final Report was published. The Labour party's early promotion of all-women shortlists resulted in 101 women becoming Labour MPs when Tony Blair led it to a big victory in 1997, and now 51 per cent of Labour MPs are women (Table 3.1). David Cameron succeeded in diversifying candidate selection in the Conservative party. When he became leader after the 2005 election, the Conservatives had only 17 women MPs; 87 Conservative women were elected in 2019. Even though the female leader of the Liberal Democrat party lost her seat in 2019, seven of its 11 MPs are women. The substantial presence of women in the Commons has led to significant changes affecting all MPs, such as the adoption of more family-friendly hours for the conduct of parliamentary business.

All parties have policies against discriminating on grounds of sexual orientation in the choice of parliamentary candidates, but they do not actively promote the adoption of lesbian, gay, bisexual or transgender

Table 3.1 How MPs represent society

	MPs Con. %	Labour %	Total %	Society %
Women	24	51	34	51
Black, Asian, Other Ethnic	6	20	10	14
Middle-class	99.4	98.5	98	37
Graduates	89	87	88	20

Source House of Commons Library Briefing Paper CBP 8749: 46ff.

candidates. Nor did the Speaker's Conference on Parliamentary Representation make proposals concerning sexuality. The Parliament elected in 2019 had a record number of MPs, 50, who were 'out', that is, publicly identified as lesbian, gay or bisexual. As the largest party in the House of Commons, the Conservatives had 23 MPs in this group; Labour had 16 and the Scottish National Party 10. Their presence has given voice in Parliament to issues such as health and social care services for LGBT individuals (https://github.com/johnpeart/lgbt-mp/).

The category of Black, Asian and minority ethnic groups combines MPs who differ in race, religion, their own or their parents' country of origin and their preferred identity. Common usage of the compound term BAME refers to what these MPs have in common: they are among the 14 per cent of Britons who are not White. However, non-White MPs are heterogeneous in terms of their ethnic identities; these include MPs of African descent, those with ancestry from diverse countries in the Indian subcontinent, Asia and the West Indies, and mixed-race offspring of White and non-White parents.

The multiracial character of British society was made present in the House of Commons in 1987 when four Black, Asian and minority ethnic Labour MPs were elected; the first Conservative BAME member was elected in 1992. The size of the group has grown at each election since, and 65 BAME MPs were elected in 2019. One-fifth of Labour MPs are now categorized as BAME compared to 6 per cent of Conservatives. Since a big majority of BAME voters favour Labour, the proportions are approximately in line with voting patterns and BAME presence in Labour constituencies. By contrast, the rise in Conservative MPs in this group from two in 2005 to 22 in 2019 has occurred because constituency parties with heavily White electorates such as Windsor have chosen BAME candidates. Boris Johnson's Cabinet has more BAME members than their proportion in the population, and more women than Blair's first Cabinet. The media usually identifies BAME MPs by their party label; for example, Rishi Sunak is referred to as the Conservative Chancellor of the Exchequer and Diane Abbott as a pro-Corbyn Labour MP.

British society has always been divided by class, but the definition of class has altered and so too has the class composition of parliamentary parties. The parliamentary Labour party historically consisted of two distinct groups: a substantial number of working-class MPs, many sponsored by the miners' and railwaymen's unions, and a professional middle class. In the 1959 Parliament, 90 Labour MPs were manual workers; the number was down to four by 2017. Traditionally Conservative MPs came from a 'well-bred' high-status background or were upper middle-class professionals or independently wealthy. Today, more Conservative MPs come from a career in business than from high-status occupations such as the law or military officers. Although upwards of two-fifths of the electorate is working-class, today less than 1 per cent of MPs have come from a working-class occupation.

In both parties working in politically relevant occupations such as party official, journalist, local government councillor, policy researcher or trade union official is now especially important for becoming an MP. A majority of Labour MPs and 101 Conservatives made a living from politics before becoming MPs. Four of the six party leaders since 2010, David Cameron, Boris Johnson, Ed Miliband and Jeremy Corbyn, have been career politicians (Campbell and Hudson 2018: 401). MPs who had worked in jobs related to politics and government before entering the House of Commons maintain they are better qualified to understand problems of their constituents and how to get them resolved than MPs whose previous occupation did not involve contact with the government (Weinberg 2020: 70ff.).

Education has replaced occupation as the most politically salient indicator of social class. Differences in education between Conservative and Labour MPs have almost disappeared as university education has expanded. In 1951 three-quarters of Conservative MPs had a private-school education and a majority went to Oxford or Cambridge. By contrast, only one-fifth of Labour MPs shared this background. Today, 88 per cent of MPs are university graduates, and there is no significant difference between the two political parties. Moreover, the path to university has not been due to attendance at fee-paying public schools. The majority of MPs in both parties attended state comprehensive or grammar schools (House of Commons 2020b: 48).

MPs today are an educational meritocracy. Whatever their family background, they have earned a good university degree. Instead of resting on their Eton laurels, Cameron earned a first-class degree at Oxford, and Johnson just missed a first. MPs have also had an education in practical politics by gaining jobs as party officials, journalists or related occupations before being elected to the House of Commons. A consequence of the professionalization of politics is that there is now a big social difference between MPs and the people they represent. MPs are more than four times as likely to be university graduates as the electorate and far more likely to be knowledgeable about the British government than most middle-class Britons. Moreover, MPs are more likely to have an arts rather than a STEM (science, technology, engineering and mathematics) degree that politicians say is needed to deal with today's problems.

Like any other occupation, being an MP tends to create a shared identity between people in that job, irrespective of their previous occupation, gender or race. Their conversations with journalists and fellow MPs tend to be carried out in terms meaningful in Westminster, but not necessarily to their voters. Impersonal electronic communication between MPs and voters contrasts with the old practice of MPs canvassing voters by appearing personally on their doorstep. The increased differentiation between the working life of MPs and of those they represent is reflected in surveys showing that many voters, whether middle-class or working-class, now feel a lack of empathy between themselves and MPs. When asked in a Hansard Society survey (2019: 51) if they feel that parties and politicians don't care about people like themselves, 50 per cent agreed, only 21 per cent disagreed and 29 per cent had no opinion.

The social diversity of today's Parliament makes a positive contribution to democratic health when issues come before the government that are directly relevant to women, racial minorities or those with a minority sexual orientation. There are MPs present in discussions of policy who can draw on personal knowledge. However, issues that dominate the political agenda such as inflation and health care concern the majority of the population irrespective of race or gender, and MPs pay most attention to these issues regardless of their social background (Koplinskaya 2017). When there is a vote in the House of Commons, then women and men, Black and White, Oxbridge and new university graduates follow the party line and vote against each other.

3.3   Representing Voters in Parliament

Democratic political theory postulates that MPs ought to represent the interests and opinions of their voters, as this is the only way in which ordinary people can have their voice heard by the government. Rational choice economists make a similar case based on the self-interest of MPs in getting re-elected. Voters are seen as principals in a transaction in which they use their votes to buy the services of MPs to represent their views in Parliament. If MPs do not do so, they risk losing votes and their seat.

British MPs have never seen their political role simply in terms of being agents of the voters in their constituency. In the eighteenth century, Edmund Burke enunciated the classic doctrine of the role of an individual MP: to give great weight to the opinion of constituents but when this is in conflict with that of their voters, MPs should follow their own judgement. Democratization has radically altered the representative role of MPs. They may form judgements on an issue but, when it conflicts with the instructions of the party whip, MPs should follow the whip. Since the great majority of MPs represent safe seats, they have little reason to fear losing their seat by voting against the views of their constituents, whereas if they vote against their party whip on a crucial issue they could lose their seat by having the party whip withdrawn. Election manifestos offer the electorate up to a hundred policy pledges that parties cite to justify their claim that they represent their voters. However, few voters will have read the manifesto of the party they vote for, and many will have no opinion on a majority of policies detailed in a manifesto.

MPs cannot exactly reflect the views of their voters because every political issue surveys show that public opinion divides into three groups—for, against and don't know. Thus, there is often no majority opinion on an issue and, even if there is, in the first-past-the-post system hundreds of MPs do not need the support of a majority of their voters to win a plurality of their constituency's vote. Moreover, the don't knows are often the median or even the plurality group, leaving MPs to decide what government should do about a given problem. Both the Conservative and Labour parties represent combinations of voters who do not have homogeneous political views.

The division of the electorate into two groups defined by their socio-economic class has been replaced by a division of the electorate into two dimensions, one defined by economic issues and the other by social attitudes that concern moral issues such as same-sex marriage, policies on crime and multiculturalism. The empirical question facing the Conservative and Labour parties is: to what extent do supporters' attitudes on economic and social issues match the views of MPs? A major survey interviewing MPs and voters after the 2019 election provided empirical data to test the congruence of their economic and social attitudes (Bale et al. 2020). The questionnaire offered both groups five questions about economic issues in which agreement registered support for a left-wing position and five questions about social issues in which agreement endorsed conservative social attitudes.

On economic issues, the position of Labour MPs and Labour voters is very similar (Table 3.2). Both groups are solidly on the left on all five economic issues: an average of 82 per cent of each group endorses left-wing positions on varied issues concerning income, wealth and business. Differences are limited, a matter of degree, usually because Labour voters

Table 3.2 Economic attitudes of MPs and voters

	MPs	Con. Voters Per cent agree	Diff'ce	MPs	Labour Voters Per cent agree	Diff'ce
For redistributing income	24	24	0	90	72	18
Big business takes advantage of ordinary people	18	62	44	83	87	4
Ordinary people don't get fair share of wealth	23	48	25	100	87	13
One law for rich, another for the poor	5	58	53	71	88	17
Management always tries to get better of employees	5	58	53	65	76	11
Mean	15	50	35	82	82	0

Source Tim Bale et al., *Mind the Values Gap*. London: The UK in a Changing Europe, 2020, 17–18. Number of voters: 15,350; MPs: 87

are more likely than MPs to have no opinion on an issue. Once that is discounted, the 13-percentage-point difference between MPs and voters on whether ordinary people get their fair share of wealth reduces to four points: 100 per cent of Labour MPs think working people do not get their fair share of the nation's wealth as do 96 per cent of Labour voters.

Conservative MPs are just as ready to reject left-wing views about business and the economy as Labour MPs are to endorse them, but Conservative voters are divided. An average of 50 per cent endorse left-wing positions and as many as 62 per cent think big business takes advantage of ordinary people. On average there is a gap of 35 percentage points between Conservative voters and their MPs. On three attitudes—business taking advantage of people, businesses taking advantage of their employees and different laws for rich and poor—Conservative voters appear closer to Labour MPs in their attitudes than to Conservative MPs. These differences may be a product of the moment since at the 2019 election the Conservative party gained an influx of pro-Brexit former Labour supporters. The only issue on which there is agreement is in opposition to redistributing income from the better off to the worse off, an indication that, even if they distrust big business, Conservative voters regard individual income as well deserved. Conservative MPs and voters tend to agree in favouring more conservative social values. The party's voters are especially strong in their endorsement of stiffer sentences for breaking the law, teaching children obedience to authority and regretting that young people do not show respect for traditional values; an average of three-quarters endorse the five measures of conservative social attitudes (Table 3.3). A majority of Conservative MPs disagree with their voters on whether the death penalty should be re-introduced, and a plurality rather than a big majority think young people don't respect British values. The profile of attitudes in the two groups differs by 21 percentage points, significantly smaller than the gap on economic issues.

Labour MPs and voters tend to see social issues differently. Four-fifths of Labour MPs have socially liberal views while Labour voters are of two minds. An average of 44 per cent endorse 'small' conservative views, 37 per cent tend to favour the liberal alternative and the remainder have no opinion. The extent to which Labour voters endorse conservative attitudes varies with the topic. An absolute majority favour stiff sentences for those who break the law and believe children should be obedient to authority.

Table 3.3   Social attitudes of MPs and voters

	MPs	Con. Voters Per cent agree	Diff'ce	MPs	Labour Voters Per cent agree	Diff'ce
Young people don't respect traditional British values	44	85	41	5	46	41
Death penalty appropriate for some crimes	21	65	44	0	30	30
Schools should teach children obedience to authority	90	83	7	41	52	9
Censor films, magazines to uphold moral standards	50	61	11	28	38	10
Stiffer sentences for breaking laws	69	84	15	24	53	29
Mean	55	76	21	20	44	24

Source Tim Bale et al., *Mind the Values Gap*. London: The UK in a Changing Europe, 2020, 17–18. Number of voters: 15,350; MPs: 87

The healthiest form of democratic representation occurs when there is a consensus about an issue among a party's MPs plus a consensus among its voters, and the two groups share the same opinion. This condition is met by the views of Labour MPs and voters on economic issues. An average of 82 per cent of MPs endorse the left-of-centre view on five issues and an equal percentage of Labour voters do so too (Table 3.2). Since this has been Labour's position since before most of those interviewed were born, this match suggests that both Labour MPs and voters were attracted to the party because it tends to favour the economically less well-off.

When there is a consensus among a party's MPs but the party's voters are divided, political leadership can maintain democratic good health by the parliamentary party making its position clear, thereby mobilizing those who agree with it and cueing those with no opinion to follow their leaders. It will also put pressure on the minority of their supporters who disagree to show party loyalty rather than initiating a split in the party. On social issues, four-fifths of Labour MPs take a liberal view while Labour voters are divided three ways. Similarly, an average of 85 per cent of Conservative MPs are in agreement in rejecting left-of-centre economic views, while their voters are divided.

If a party's MPs are divided about issues, this is bad for democratic choice because it creates confusion about where the party stands on a particular issue and the party's manifesto may fudge the party's position on the issue. Divisions among its MPs can also lose a party's votes. At the 2019 election the Labour party, badly divided about the issue of Brexit, pledged that it would negotiate a sensible deal on Europe, without saying what that meant, and then hold a referendum so that voters could accept or reject what it did. By contrast, under Boris Johnson the Conservatives were united in campaigning to get Brexit done. Labour lost one-fifth of the vote it had won at the previous general election while the Conservatives gained their greatest share of the popular vote since 1979.

3.4   MPs Can Influence Policy but not Govern

Parliament supports British democracy by institutionalizing the accountability of government. As representatives of the electorate, MPs can hold the government of the day accountable by prodding, questioning and scrutinizing government actions on a continuing basis. Collectively, the case that government ministers make for what they are doing and the criticisms and alternatives put forward by the official Opposition party give voters help in deciding which party to endorse when the time comes to hold the government accountable at a general election.

Whatever their party, individual MPs have a wide choice of roles that they can undertake. They can specialize in causes of concern to themselves and any interest groups to which they are affiliated. Some but not all MPs seek publicity for themselves through media soundbites or income by receiving a paid retainer to represent an interest. Many MPs have ambitions to become a minister; this requires showing skill in debate and cultivating the favour of the party leader and the party whips, who assist in assigning the hundred-odd government or shadow ministerial posts. MPs who never become a minister may be satisfied with concentrating on constituency affairs.

Parliament offers many resources that MPs can use individually and collectively to hold the government of the day to account. A parliamentary question can prompt a minister to review what their department has been doing about an issue. If there is no strong partisan slant to the issue, the minister can give a friendly but vague reply. If there is a partisan slant, criticism may be met by claiming everything necessary is being done, even if some actions began only after the question was received. If an unexpected problem begins making news, MPs can question what the government will do next and in hindsight ask why it didn't act sooner and more effectively. Putting an issue on the agenda of Parliament also can attract media attention and prompt journalistic enquiries.

All-party committees of MPs identify topics that can be probed in detail by holding hearings at which MPs can question ministers, senior civil servants and outside experts with diverse views, some of which are at variance with the government of the day. Interest groups and experts are invited to submit evidence-based advice. A committee report that contains recommendations agreed by MPs of all parties will carry more weight on non-party issues. There are unofficial cross-party committees of MPs that promote issues that cut across party lines, such as disability policy or sports. Each party has a weekly meeting at which backbenchers can interrogate party leaders. The many corridors and places of refreshment within the Palace of Westminster offer opportunities for a quick word with colleagues, opponents and journalists, and MPs now use apps to co-ordinate actions to advance shared views.

When MPs question ministers, they are judging people as well as policies, for a minister's reputation depends upon being able to give a convincing account of what he or she is doing. Ministers may win a vote in the House of Commons but lose standing if they show limited understanding of the brief that civil servants have given them. A backbench MP who gets the best of ministers may be spoken of approvingly as a future minister by other MPs and journalists.

Performing well in the House of Commons is especially important for shadow ministers on the Opposition benches, for they need to convince the electorate as well as other MPs that their party is capable of governing. Jeremy Corbyn's inability to get the best of Theresa May or Boris Johnson reflected his inability to convince his own MPs or the electorate that he was fit to lead a government. By contrast, Keir Starmer has been a professional barrister, a skill peculiarly appropriate for an Opposition party. Starmer can cross-examine ministers about weaknesses and faults in their policies in an effort to demonstrate to voters that the Labour party is fit to govern.

The one thing the House of Commons cannot do is legislate; this is the job of the government. Whitehall departments, in consultation with ministers, prepare the several dozen bills that are presented to Parliament annually. Some are published in draft form to flush out difficulties that may be revised before their formal introduction in the Commons. Interested MPs can ask probing questions about features of the bill that are unclear or ill-thought-out in hopes that the government will alter how it works. Amendments can be moved by the Opposition, by a group of backbench MPs or by the government itself. Amendments that the government opposes are almost invariably defeated. On rare occasions parliamentary scrutiny can reveal faults that lead the government to withdraw a bill. Many government blunders have their origins in Acts of Parliament that have been scrutinized by MPs and even enacted without opposition.

An MP can refuse to follow the party whip on grounds of political principle, personal conscience or constituency concerns, by abstaining or even voting against the party line. However, such occasions are rare; in both parties a majority of MPs never vote against their party's whip in the course of a parliamentary year (www. publicwhip.org). In ten years Blair's government was only defeated four times (en.wikipedia.org/wiki/List_of_government_defeats_in_the_ House_of_Commons_(1945–present)). When Brexit was a divisive issue in the 2015–2017 Parliament, Johnson did not vote even once against the line taken by May's government. Outspoken EU rebels such as Jacob Rees-Mogg voted with the government in 98.2 per cent of all divisions and Kenneth Clarke in 95.6 per cent.

After the Conservative government of Theresa May became a minority government in 2017, the House of Commons demonstrated that the one thing it cannot do is make government policy. The chief issue facing the government was how to implement Brexit, which an all-party parliamentary majority had accepted. MPs of all parties combined to reject by up to 432 votes the agreement to implement Brexit that May had made with the EU. MPs negotiated within and across party lines to formulate proposals for making a bigger or lesser break with the European Union or holding a 'think again' referendum to reverse the decision to leave the EU. Sir Bill Cash, a Conservative MP who had campaigned against the EU for decades, denounced such activities as unconstitutional attempts to create a government by Parliament.

When groups of MPs put forward 15 different proposals for implementing Brexit between January and October 2019, all 15 were rejected by margins ranging from 6 to 313 (Rose 2020: Table 11). Boris Johnson succeeded in breaking the impasse between a government that couldn't govern and a Parliament that couldn't govern by calling a general election. To ensure that a Conservative majority in Parliament would back whatever he negotiated with Brussels, Johnson made unprecedented use of party discipline. He expelled 21 Conservative MPs, and all of these who sought re-election were defeated. To make sure that all Tory MPs in the new Parliament would endorse whatever Downing Street decided, each Conservative candidate had to give a written personal pledge to vote for whatever Johnson recommended to get Brexit done. Every Tory MP did so and promptly after the election the United Kingdom left the European Union.

Parties have made a positive contribution to the health of British democracy by nominating MPs who not only reflect political divisions in the electorate on economic issues but also the diversity of British society today in terms of gender, race and minority ethnic status. Parties have succeeded in integrating MPs and voters from diverse backgrounds because of their shared political values and interests. Parliament keeps up a healthy pressure on the government to give an account of its activities. Individual MPs have many opportunities to prod and criticize the government, and the Opposition party has opportunities to stake its claim to being better able to govern than the party controlling the government of the day. Thus, when a general election comes, voters are not confronted with candidates who have not been seen debating government policies for the previous five years, as happens in presidential systems such as the United States. The inability of MPs to agree with a policy to implement Brexit is not a sign of political ill health but a reminder that Britain does not have a system of parliamentary government but of representative government. It is MPs' role to hold Cabinet ministers to account by raising questions and presenting criticisms that represent alternatives to policies being made in Whitehall.

REFERENCES

Bale, Tim, A. Cheung, P. Cowley, A. Menon, and A. Wager. 2020. *Mind the Values Gap*. London: The UK in a Changing Europe.

Campbell, Rosie, and Jennifer Hudson. 2018. Political Recruitment Under Pressure. In Philip Cowley and Dennis Kavanagh, *The British General Election of 2017*, 385–408. London: Palgrave Macmillan.

Criddle, Byron. 2016. Variable Diversity: MPs and Candidates. In Philip Cowley and Dennis Kavanagh, *The British General Election of 2015*, 336–360. London: Palgrave Macmillan.

Hansard Society. 2019. *Audit of Political Engagement 16*. London: Hansard Society.

House of Commons. 2010. *Speaker's Conference on Parliamentary Representation: Final Report*. London: Stationary Office, HC 239-1.

House of Commons. 2020a. *General Election 2019: Results and Analysis*. London: House of Commons Library Briefing Paper CBP 8749.

House of Commons. 2020b. *UK Election Statistics: 1918–2019: A Century of Elections*, 2nd ed. London: House of Commons Briefing Paper CBP 7529.

Koplinskaya, E. 2017. Substantive Representation in the UK Parliament. *Parliamentary Affairs 70*: 111–131.

Phillips, Anne. 1995. *The Politics of Presence*. Oxford: Oxford University Press.

Rose, Richard. 1989. *Politics in England*, 5th ed. London: Macmillan.

Rose, Richard. 2020. *How Referendums Challenge European Democracy: Brexit and Beyond*. London: Palgrave Macmillan.

Weinberg, James. 2020. *Who Enters Politics and Why?*. Bristol: Bristol University Press.

CHAPTER 4

A Single Brain in Downing Street

The prime minister is the head of the body politic; this is a far stronger position than simply being the first among equals chairing Cabinet meetings. Because the system of party government fuses Parliament and government, there is a single brain at the head of the British body politic. By contrast, the president of the United States is head of the executive branch but must rely on the Senate and the House of Representatives for approval of legislation, the budget and presidential appointees. It took four Democratic Party presidents more than half a century to get the great majority of Americans covered by health insurance. In Britain it took the Labour government of Clement Attlee three years to establish a national health service.

Television has made the prime minister the face of government. By definition, anything connected with Number 10 is newsworthy, even the antics of the occupant's dog or cat if there is one. Whether the prime minister has a striking personality or not, no other national politician can compete for attention with him or her. In 2018 Theresa May, whose shoes were more colourful than her personality, produced a dozen times more Google results than the leader of the Opposition, Jeremy Corbyn. Although television beams pictures of the prime minister getting in and out of a car outside Number 10, we don't see what goes on behind its front door.

R. Rose, *How Sick Is British Democracy?*
Challenges to Democracy in the 21st Century,
https://doi.org/10.1007/978-3-030-73123-6_4

Although the prime minister has only one brain, he or she has two hats, one as party leader and the other as the chief maker of government decisions. As party leader, the prime minister must generate enough popular approval to secure the party's electoral fortunes. As head of government, the prime minister must make decisions that balance competing claims from Cabinet ministers reflecting their departmental interests. They must also maintain personal popularity and support for the party in opinion polls and guard themselves from Cabinet colleagues who are ambitious to become prime minister sooner rather than later.

Diagnosing the political health of the occupants of Downing Street requires an understanding of the process by which an ambitious politician becomes their party's leader. A politician successful in becoming prime minister then faces a very different challenge: making selective decisions that only the prime minister can make. One sign of prime ministerial health is that he or she maintains the confidence of both their MPs and the British electorate. It is also a sign of good health that, if a party leader loses party and popular confidence, he or she is promptly removed from office.

Because the prime minister, like the occupant of the White House, is the public face of government, this is sometimes claimed to have created an unhealthy concentration of power by making the occupant of Downing Street a president. However, the media visibility of the two officeholders co-exists with fundamental differences in the political institutions of which their offices are a part (see Rose 2001: 236–244). A prime minister heads the party that controls Parliament and governs without the checks of a written constitution and of federal partners. By contrast, the American president can be checked by Congress and by the courts. Moreover, Donald Trump learned that the federal system results in the states controlling the conduct of elections and deciding the winner.

4.1   PARTIES DECIDE WHO CAN BECOME PRIME MINISTER

While popular votes decide which party governs, it is the winning party that chooses which MP becomes prime minister. Their name is not on the ballot in 649 of the United Kingdom's 650 constituencies. When a new party leader is chosen by a party in government, party members, 1 per cent or less of the electorate, can make the choice.

The Conservative and Labour parties have tried three different methods for electing their party leaders since 1965. The changes have progressively reduced the role of MPs and increased the influence of party members. Each party has a two-stage process. MPs nominate candidates and then hold elimination ballots to select the top two MPs, whose names are then put to the party membership for the final decision. In choosing a party leader, members can give priority to the candidate they think most likely to lead the party to an election victory or to the candidate who most represents their shade of partisanship. Party members have less knowledge of the demands of government than do MPs.

Because the prime minister must be a member of the House of Commons, the first step for an aspiring politician is to be selected at a young age as a parliamentary candidate in a constituency in which the party has a hefty majority. Tony Blair, Gordon Brown, Jeremy Corbyn, David Cameron and Boris Johnson were between 30 and 35 when they first became MPs. This gave each of them a head start in achieving their ambitions over the majority of MPs, who do not enter the House of Commons until they are in their 40s or older. Keir Starmer is unusual in not becoming an MP until he was 54 years old.

Once in Parliament, ambitious young MPs need to start building a reputation among their fellow MPs, in the media and among party members nationwide by standing out in parliamentary debate and by supporting the party leadership. There are a variety of ways in which MPs can put themselves in the running to lead the party. After Oxford, David Cameron began building his career as a Conservative party researcher.

Theresa May became a shadow minister within a year of entering the House of Commons and rose to prominence as Home Secretary in Cameron's Cabinet. Boris Johnson gained a reputation as an election-winner by being elected mayor of Greater London. Jeremy Corbyn gained support among the Labour party's left-wing members by frequently rebelling against the Labour whip.

The criteria that the party's selectorate uses to choose a leader depend upon circumstances. When a party is in opposition, a successful leadership candidate needs to look like an election-winner. One way to do so is to have an appeal that is similar to that of the prime minister. Thus, when 44-year-old Tony Blair ended 18 years of Conservative government in 1997, the 36-year-old William Hague jumped over his seniors to become party leader. With Blair in his third term in Downing Street, the Conservatives chose the 39-year-old David Cameron as the leader to give the party a fresh face rather than a leader associated with Margaret Thatcher's term in office. An alternative strategy is to choose a party leader who offers a clear contrast. Conservative MPs chose John Major to succeed Thatcher as prime minister because he was not a dominant personality nor did he offer a 'Majorist' ideology after a decade of Thatcher and Thatcherism.

When the party is in government an MP can become prime minister because of their experience in holding senior Cabinet posts: this helped both Jim Callaghan and Theresa May get to the top. Alternatively, if the governing party's prospect for re-election is bad, then winning votes can take precedence over ministerial performance. Boris Johnson became the party's prime minister in July 2019 with the combined support of Conservatives who favoured him in the belief he would both deliver Brexit and a general election victory and of those who were opposed to Brexit and distrusted Johnson personally but believed he would be an election-winner.

To become party leader, ambition is not enough: an MP needs to have luck for the leadership to become vacant at a time when their political star is in the ascendant. The breakdown in the health of Prime Minister Anthony Eden after the Suez War gave Harold Macmillan the unexpected opportunity to become Conservative prime minister in 1957. The road to Downing Street was opened for Harold Wilson by the death of Hugh Gaitskell in 1963, and for Tony Blair in 1994 when the death of John Smith created the opportunity to lead the Labour party.

The fastest way to become prime minister is to be chosen leader of a party when it is in government. Since 1945, 10 of Britain's 15 prime ministers have entered Downing Street as the choice of a selectorate within their party rather than of the electorate. All 10 had headed at least one major government department, the Treasury, the Foreign Office or the Home Office; Harold Macmillan and John Major had held two; and Jim Callaghan all three.

Four senior politicians gained Downing Street to prevent a Cabinet colleague from becoming prime minister. Thus, Sir Alec Douglas-Home was named prime minister because Conservative grandees did not want R. A. Butler to get the post, and Jim Callaghan took the highest office to stop Michael Foot from becoming Labour prime minister. John Major benefited by being the opponent of Michael Heseltine, who had divided Conservative MPs by challenging Prime Minister Margaret Thatcher. When Boris Johnson and Michael Gove disagreed about who should be the pro-Brexit candidate to succeed David Cameron, this gave Theresa May the opportunity to become prime minister.

A politician who becomes a party leader in opposition faces an uphill task. An immediate need is to establish his or her authority over colleagues who have been competitors by offering them the shadow patronage of being a shadow Cabinet minister. The new leader's starting point for winning a general election is to gain recognition from the electorate that he or she is a potential prime minister, while lacking the media attention and aura that go with actually being prime minister.

Of the 13 Opposition party leaders since 1950, eight have failed to enter Downing Street and five have succeeded.

Three Conservatives who became the leader in opposition have succeeded in forming a government. Ted Heath won an upset victory against Harold Wilson in 1970; Margaret Thatcher gained office from a Labour government that was discredited by economic stagflation; and David Cameron did the same in 2010. The youthful William Hague was the first Conservative Opposition leader to challenge Tony Blair unsuccessfully. Hague's successor, Iain Duncan Smith, appeared so inadequate that Conservative MPs secured his resignation before he could lead the party to defeat in the 2005 election. Michael Howard dutifully undertook that task.

Two Labour leaders after Clement Attlee have entered Downing Street by winning a general election as leader of the Opposition. Harold Wilson won a very narrow victory in the 1964 general election after inheriting from Hugh Gaitskell a big lead over a Macmillan government in deep trouble. Similarly, Labour was well ahead of a Conservative government discredited by a fall in the value of the pound when Blair become Labour leader in 1994. Blair exploited the party's thirst for regaining office after four successive defeats by transforming the party's image. To paraphrase the recipe for success of Elvis Presley's manager, he was a 'red boy who could sing blue'. Five Labour Opposition leaders have failed to win a general election: Hugh Gaitskell, Michael Foot, Neil Kinnock twice, Ed Miliband, and Jeremy Corbyn twice.

The system of choosing party leaders is in good health if the party's MPs and members agree about who should be their leader. Since 2001 Conservative party members have been eligible to participate in the election of four party leaders. The membership's choice in 2001 of Iain Duncan Smith instead of the MPs' favourite, Kenneth Clarke, was rectified in 2003 by Conservative MPs pushing Duncan Smith out and installing a different leader, Michael Howard, without a contest, thereby ruling out the prospect of a clash between MPs and party members in the choice of leader. Subsequently, David Cameron and Boris Johnson were endorsed as leaders by both MPs and party members, while MPs elected Theresa May as a leader without opposition.

The Labour leader was the first choice of MPs as well as of the unions and constituency parties in each election from 1983 up to 2010, when symptoms of ill health began to appear. In 2010 the trade union vote made Ed Miliband party leader against the MPs' endorsement of his brother David. In 2015 Jeremy Corbyn had the endorsement of only 15 per cent of Labour MPs but won the party leadership by the vote of the mass membership. Immediately following the Brexit referendum, Labour MPs voted no confidence in Corbyn by a margin of 172 to 40. However, Corbyn dismissed the MPs' action because he was elected their leader by party members. In 2020 Keir Starmer became the first Labour leader since Tony Blair to win the vote of the party's MPs and its membership, as Gordon Brown had become Labour prime minister without a contest in 2007.

It is a sign of democratic good health that the prime minister's party should sometimes win re-election but not all the time. By this standard, the British system appears healthy. In the 20 elections since 1950, voters have eight times confirmed their initial choice by re-electing the incumbent prime minister to another term. In an additional six elections, voters have re-elected the government under a new prime minister chosen by the governing party during the life of a Parliament. Three prime ministers—Clement Attlee, Winston Churchill and Ted Heath—have won at least one election and lost at least one. Three leaders chosen by their party when it was the government—Sir Alec Douglas-Home, Jim Callaghan and Gordon Brown—served as prime minister but were rejected by the electorate when they sought its endorsement.

4.2   What a Prime Minister Can and Can't Do

The job of a prime minister is radically different from that of an MP or a journalist. Instead of talking about what government ought to do, the prime minister is uniquely responsible for what government does. Every problem facing a prime minister is both an impersonal issue of policy and a personal political challenge. The impersonal question is: 'What should the government do?' The personal question is: 'What effect will what I do have on my political capital?' Policy is both an end in itself and a means of maintaining a hold on Downing Street. The unique loneliness of the job at the top of the British government makes every temporary holder of the office a Marxist in Groucho's sense: 'Take care of me. I'm the only one I've got'.

The prime minister must take decisions that only the head of government can make. Many are meta-decisions resolving disagreements between ministers with different departmental interests, such as disputes between the Treasury and health, education and pensions ministers about the amount the government should spend on social policies. A prime minister is ex officio involved in phone calls and meetings with heads of other governments about problems, such as civil wars on other continents, that the British government can do little to affect.

The life-threatening coronavirus pandemic is a textbook example of an event placing multiple pressures on the prime minister. There are daily briefings on the up-and-down statistics about controlling the virus. There are briefings from civil servants about difficulties in implementing decisions in the limbs and hands of the body politic. Meta-decisions are needed to resolve conflicts between ministers wanting to minimize the costs of locking down the economy and health ministers pushing for lockdowns to minimize the loss of lives. The prime minister appears on television to explain government's shifting responses and to appeal for popular co-operation. By flanking himself with government scientific advisers, Johnson gives the impression that he is following 'the science'. However, as Newton (2020: 506) notes, 'When you cross politics with science, what you get is politics'.

The fundamental dilemma facing prime ministers is that, while their formal responsibilities are vast, there are not enough hours in the week to deal with all of them. Their policymaking activities are governed by the rule of first things first. The constraints of the clock result in a prime minister engaging in management by exception, setting aside or ignoring the bulk of policies for which he or she is nominally accountable. Prime ministers can and do take selective initiatives that impact their reputation for better or for worse. Margaret Thatcher made a mark by selling council houses to tenants and privatizing nationalized industries. She is also remembered for introducing the poll tax, a policy that led to her downfall. Tony Blair was determined to bring about a political settlement in Northern Ireland, and the 1998 Good Friday Agreement ended three decades of deadly conflict. He was also responsible, without consulting the Cabinet, for Britain invading Iraq as a junior partner of the United States, with far more lethal results.

The memoirs of politicians are revealing in what they omit as well as what they include. Every prime minister's memoir is full of detailed discussions of foreign affairs, economic difficulties, personal initiatives and select and often unwelcome events. They pay little or no attention to the activities of a majority of departments that collectively consume most of the public expenditure, such as pensions and social security. For example, in Ted Heath's memoirs, each of the indexed references to health refers to Heath's personal health, such as injuring his leg in a sailing race; none refers to the National Health Service. When the prime minister offers an MP a Cabinet post, little or no direction may be given about what should be done beyond what is in the party's manifesto.

The great volume of public policies is in the first instance the responsibility of Cabinet ministers. Inter-departmental issues can be dealt with through Cabinet committees and, if the issue is politically charged, by the prime minister. Prime ministers have varied in how they deal with Cabinet. Clement Attlee gave priority to balancing the views of politically important Cabinet ministers rather than trying to give them direction. One of Attlee's mottos was, 'If you have a good dog, don't bark yourself'. Jim Callaghan put minimizing friction between Cabinet ministers first when his government faced the prospect of imposing economic austerity as a condition of an IMF loan in 1976. He let ministers with opposing views argue their case in Cabinet and then sided with the most vigorous proponent, Chancellor of the Exchequer Denis Healey. By contrast, before asking ministers to state their views, Margaret Thatcher often began a discussion by telling ministers what she thought ought to be done. Like Thatcher, Gordon Brown was prepared to read in detail documents on topics that require prime ministerial attention. Downing Street has told officials that if they want their briefings to be read by Boris Johnson they should keep them short, preferably one page. He has also made clear that the fewer meta-policy decisions he has to take about wicked issues in which all choices are unpalatable, the more comfortable he feels with the job of prime minister.

For decades after the Second World War, prime ministers relied on the institutions of the Cabinet government to exert their influence on what the government did (see Rose 2001: Chapter 8). Prime ministers had the same number of special assistants that President Franklin D. Roosevelt had when he promoted the American New Deal, four, and the civil service jealously sought to maintain its virtual monopoly of posts in Downing Street. Ted Heath's chief economic adviser in opposition could not have a desk in Downing Street, and his political private secretary was charged for postage stamps. Harold Wilson began the practice of bringing into Downing Street a journalist and a political secretary to support his personal political position.

The capacity of the prime minister to give direction to the government changed in 1997 when Blair became prime minister with the announced aim of creating a New Britain. He brought with him two key advisers from his time in opposition: Jonathan Powell, an ex-diplomat, as his chief adviser for policy and Alastair Campbell, a *Daily Mirror* journalist, as press secretary. Blair wanted each to be given the authority to direct civil servants, conventionally the exclusive preserve of ministers. The head of the civil service grudgingly gave approval. Powell was put in charge of a unit to provide Blair with briefings on policy and giving guidance to departments about what Downing Street wanted. Blair preferred 'sofa government'—informal discussions about policies with his advisers and without civil servants taking minutes—to well-prepared Cabinet meetings in which ministers could present diverse departmental views about an issue. Cabinet meetings were reduced to less than one a week and some lasted no more than an hour. Notwithstanding the interdependence of the Chancellor of the Exchequer's economic policy and the prime minister's election strategy, relations between Blair and his Chancellor, Gordon Brown, were strained as Brown believed he was better qualified to be prime minister and jealously protected his powers.

Blair sought to be accountable to the electorate through the media rather than through Parliament or the Labour party and assigned Alastair Campbell the job of 'making' the news. The strategy gives priority to presenting policies first to the media rather than the House of Commons, relying on the media to lead its report with the government's favourable story rather than give a balanced account including criticisms from Opposition MPs. Bad news was released, if possible, when the House of Commons was not sitting. Questions about unpopular policies could be countered by distracting facts or dismissed with no comment. Interviews were given to journalists who would report the prime minister's views sympathetically in return for receiving exclusive access.

Like Blair, Johnson has surrounded himself in Number 10 with congenial policy advisers who will support his campaigning instincts. Of the 11 persons listed in a press profile of 'Boris Johnson's new power hub', most were from the media and only two were Cabinet ministers: the Chancellor of the Exchequer Rishi Sunak and Michael Gove, Johnson's Brexit ally (Shipman 2020). The majority of Johnson's Cabinet ministers whose departments do not deal with his priority concerns have been said to have 'to look in the mirror in the morning to check that they exist' (Kempsell 2020). Backbench Tory MPs, whose support is needed in an internal party vote of confidence, feel neglected and can brief journalists about their dissatisfactions. In the words of the vice president of the 1922 Committee of Conservative MPs, 'If you keep whacking a dog, don't be surprised when it bites you back' (Parker and Payne 2020).

Having made a career writing opinion pieces as a journalist, Boris Johnson has given priority to using the media, rather than Parliament or party institutions, to communicate with voters. Unlike Harold Wilson, who used private briefings with print journalists to get his views put forward and Donald Trump who distrusted the media and relied on tweeting, Johnson has relied on television. The coronavirus pandemic has given him an unprecedented opportunity to appear frequently in daily press conferences briefing the public on issues of wide public concern. When these end, he planned to launch a daily televised press conference from a new £2.6 studio in Downing Street in which an experienced television journalist would present the prime minister's views directly to a mass audience rather than have Downing Street's words edited by print journalists. When Johnson faced difficult questions from journalists about spending on furnishing his Downing Street flat, the plan for a daily press conference was abandoned.

Unlike Blair, Johnson has little interest in engaging with policymaking. As the threat of a COVID-19 pandemic built up, Johnson did not bother to chair the COBRA (Cabinet Office Briefing Rooms) meetings preparing emergency plans. He gave his chief policy adviser Dominic Cummings the authority to transform what Cummings dismissed as the Whitehall blob. Cummings started to create a Whitehall unit to monitor government policymaking with computers and dashboards. It was modelled on the Advanced Research Projects Agency of the Pentagon, which uses innovative electronic technology for national security projects and moon shots. Instead of relying on the usual cadre of policy advisers (see Chapter 5), Cummings advertised for 'weirdos and misfits with odd skills' to join his new unit (https://dominiccummings.com/2020/01/02/).

A sign of Johnson's dependence on others to look after what was happening in Whitehall departments was given when Cummings violated the government's coronavirus stay-at-home policy in late March 2020. Although two government scientific advisers had been summarily dropped when their violations became public, when the media revealed that Cummings had done so, Johnson let Cummings use the Number 10 rose garden to defend himself without apology. When Johnson was asked whether he stood by Cummings or the British people, Johnson replied, 'My choice is the choice of the British people.' A YouGov survey found that 59 per cent of the British people thought that Cummings should resign; he did not. However, by November 2020, Cummings' use of power made him so many enemies in Downing Street; he was forced to resign and has since attacked Johnson for abusing prime ministerial power.

The form and size of the prime minister's political support vary with personal and political characteristics of the prime minister. The technocratic Ted Heath established the Central Policy Review Staff to provide himself and Cabinet ministers with a longer term independent perspective on policy than was normally found in Whitehall departments. Margaret Thatcher (1993: 30) abolished it on the grounds that its technocratic approach was unsuitable for a government that had 'a firm philosophical direction' and 'knew what it wanted to do'. Tony Blair preferred to rely on special advisers whom he trusted personally and consulted informally. Boris Johnson would prefer to delegate engagement with the details of government policy but the coronavirus pandemic has forced him to engage with expert advisers before taking critical decisions balancing the deadly threat it poses to citizens and the costly threat it poses to the British economy.

It is a symptom of political bad health when a prime minister enters Downing Street with no experience of heading a large government department. When Blair became prime minister in 1997, he became the first prime minister who had never been a Cabinet minister since Ramsay Macdonald in 1923. Reflecting on what he had learned about his experience of government two years in office, Blair said, 'You try getting change in the public sector and the public services. I bear the scars on my back' (quoted in Rose 2001: 156). During his short tenure as foreign secretary, Boris Johnson gave more thought to becoming prime minister than to learning how to manage a Whitehall department.

4.3   PERSONALITY CONSTANT, POPULARITY FLUCTUATES

The personalities of prime ministers vary widely within parties. No Conservative would ever confuse John Major and Boris Johnson and no Labour supporter would confuse Tony Blair and Gordon Brown. However, the personality of a prime minister is shaped long before he or she enters the House of Commons. The character of Theresa May or Boris Johnson as prime minister is recognizable in accounts given by their Oxford contemporaries of their time there. Becoming prime minister gives their personality an aura, but it does not change who they are as individuals.

A party leader is often referred to as having a charismatic personality, but this is misleading. The German sociologist Max Weber (1958) borrowed the term from theology to describe leaders with characters so exceptional that they can disrupt institutions and gain power in their own name. It fittingly describes such historical personages as Napoleon, Adolf Hitler and Charles de Gaulle. The failure of British politicians with a disruptive character shows the strength of the institutions of British democracy. Enoch Powell had a striking personality, but when he stood for the Conservative leadership in 1965 only 15 of his fellow MPs voted for him. From 1968 onwards, when he decried immigration as threatening 'rivers of blood' in British streets, public opinion polls gave Powell a very high rating as a personality. Before the February 1974 general election, Powell's anti-European Union views led him to vote for the Labour party, which was then anti-EU. He ended his parliamentary career as a backbench Ulster Unionist MP.

Nigel Farage projected a striking personality and achieved exceptional success in campaigning for Britain to leave the European Union but he failed in seven attempts to win a seat in the House of Commons as an anti-EU party candidate. Conservative prime ministers disrupted Farage's party by stealing his signature policy, Brexit.

For three-quarters of a century surveys have been asking the British public to evaluate prime ministers. Beginning with Clement Attlee in 1945, the Gallup Poll frequently asked: *Are you satisfied or dissatisfied with ... as Prime Minister?* By the time Gallup stopped its trend polling, Ipsos MORI was asking: *Are you satisfied or dissatisfied with the way ... is doing his/her job as Prime Minister?* Altogether, upwards of 700 surveys provide evidence of the popularity of 15 prime ministers differing in personality, party and electoral success.

Democratic prime ministers cannot expect to enjoy the 100 per cent approval that dictators claim, because they must compete with leaders of other parties for public favour. Nor can a British prime minister claim to speak for the whole of the country as can the French president, who is both an elected politician and the ceremonial head of state. Least of all can a prime minister claim to be a symbol of national unity like Queen Elizabeth II.

In keeping with being a leader who must compete for office, more than four-fifths of prime ministers have had their satisfaction rating average below 50 per cent. The median prime ministers, Alec Douglas-Home and Harold Wilson during his initial six years in office, were approved by an average of 45 per cent of Gallup Poll respondents (Table 4.1). The highest average rating, 57 per cent, was achieved by Anthony Eden, since he quickly left office after the failure of his abortive attempt to seize the Suez Canal. The satisfaction of just over half with Churchill shows that even a politician with a wartime claim to be the nation's leader (average wartime rating: 87 per cent approval) is evaluated as a party politician in

Table 4.1 Prime ministers vary in popularity

	Low	Average (Per cent approving)	High
Eden	41	57	73
Macmillan	30	52	79
Churchill	48	52	56
Blair	23	49	75
Attlee	37	47	66
Callaghan	33	46	59
Wilson, 1974–1976	40	46	53
Wilson, 1964–1970	27	45	69
Douglas-Home	40	45	48
Johnson	33	42	52
Cameron	28	42	57
May	26	41	56
Thatcher	23	39	53
Heath	31	37	45
Brown	21	31	41
Major	17	28	59

Sources Attlee to Major: Gallup Poll (King and Wybrow 2001: 183–198). Blair to Johnson: Ipsos MORI Political Monitor (https://www.ipsos.com/ipsos-mori/en-uk/political-monitor-archive)

peacetime (average approval 52 per cent). Harold Macmillan was unusual in sustaining his popularity during seven years in office.

Four prime ministers have each had an average satisfaction rating below 40 per cent—Margaret Thatcher 39 per cent, Ted Heath 37 per cent, Gordon Brown 31 per cent and John Major 28 per cent. These low ratings have not doomed them to electoral defeat. Thatcher won all three elections she fought; Heath won his first election and lost the next two; and Major won his first election too before falling victim to the collapse of sterling and losing in his bid for re-election. Gordon Brown lost the only election he fought as prime minister.

Since the swinging 1960s there has been a big shift in media coverage of prime ministers from the deferential treatment of the BBC to aggressive questioning by television interviewers. Print media have changed from describing politicians as Mr Attlee and Mr. Macmillan to headlining their personal and political flaws and satirizing them on the cover of *Private Eye*. However, there is no evidence of a downward trend in prime ministerial approval. Tony Blair, who was not even born when Clement Attlee was prime minister, had a higher approval rating than Attlee and Harold Wilson. Theresa May, who wasn't even born when Winston Churchill was last prime minister, had the same approval rating that he did.

The chief fluctuation in the popularity of prime ministers occurs within their term of office. On entering Downing Street, a prime minister is likely to have a high level of approval. It then slumps as a consequence of taking decisions deemed necessary but unpopular, or due to making avoidable mistakes. As the next election casts a shadow forwards, a prime minister will alter tactics in an effort to boost popularity. The net effect of the cycle of ups and downs in monthly ratings is that there is usually no significant trend up or down during a prime minister's term of office (Rose 1995: Table 2).

Four-fifths of prime ministers have had popular approval rise above 50 per cent at some point of their time in office (Fig. 4.1). Macmillan achieved the highest rating on record, 79 per cent in 1960, eight months after his general election triumph. Blair achieved the second-highest rating, 75 per cent approval, shortly after his initial election victory in 1997. The three prime ministers who never had the approval of half the public—Brown, Heath and Douglas-Home—were each one-term prime ministers.

Being popular does not protect a prime minister from becoming unpopular, and 11 have seen their satisfaction rating fall to 33 per cent or

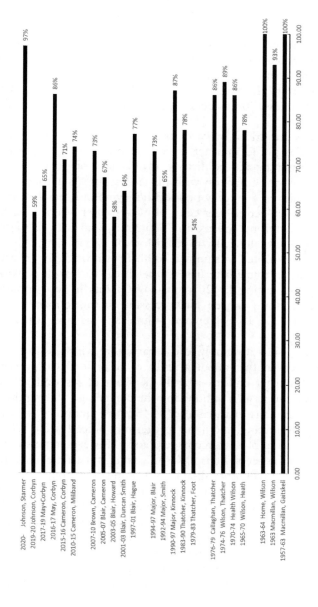

Fig. 4.1 Combined approval of major party leaders (*Note* Leadership rating combines average support for Prime Minister and Leader of Opposition. Calculated by the author from sources in Tables 4.1 and 4.2)

less at some point in their term of office. When Tony Blair entered Downing Street, his campaign Svengali Peter Mandelson boasted that there would be no mid-term slump. However, satisfaction with Blair fluctuated by 52 percentage points from its monthly high to its low. Blair's average approval dropped during each of his terms in office. It was 53 per cent in his first term, 36 per cent in his second and 29 per cent in his third and final term. During 11 years in office, Margaret Thatcher's popularity fluctuated less, 30 percentage points, because she was never so popular as Blair.

Approval ratings are driven more by the performance of the government for which the prime minister is responsible than by the stable personality of late-middle-age politicians. Blair's decision to go to war in Iraq created mass dissatisfaction with his leadership. As a contrast to Thatcher, Major enjoyed a lengthy political honeymoon in his first term of office; approval averaged 49 per cent. However, after Major won the April 1992 election, sterling collapsed in September and with it Major's popularity; it continued falling, to a record low of 17 per cent. When a global banking crisis erupted in summer 2008, Brown used his Treasury experience to bring an immediate halt to the threat to British banking, boosting his approval rating by 20 percentage points in four months. However, as the economy moved into recession in the following year, Brown's approval fell by 15 percentage points, and he was headed to electoral defeat.

British prime ministers invariably lead a party that wins less than half the popular vote. Given that about a tenth of respondents express no opinion, a prime minister endorsed by 45 per cent of respondents can have a net approval rating after subtracting the percentage voicing disapproval (Table 4.1). For two decades after 1945 prime ministers normally had a positive approval rating, and in his first term of office Harold Wilson had a net approval rating of 27 percentage points. However, after sterling was devalued early in his second term Wilson's rating turned negative and from 1966 to 1970 he had a net disapproval rating of 6 points. During Ted Heath's term of office, an average of 51 per cent voiced their disapproval, giving him a net disapproval rating of four percentage points. After returning to office in 1974 Wilson recovered to gain a net approval rating of two percentage points, and his successor, Jim Callaghan, had a net approval rating of five percentage points.

Net disapproval by the electorate need not prevent a prime minister from winning re-election. Thatcher's strong convictions produced a strong reaction for and against her, resulting in those disapproving outnumbering her admirers in each of her terms in office. Nonetheless, she twice won re-election. During Major's first term of office, he had a net approval rating of +18 per cent, but after the pound crashed it immediately turned negative and reached a record low of −59 per cent in August 1994. Blair ended his first term in office with a net approval rating of 21 per cent, but in his second term his rating reversed, with 54 per cent expressing disapproval compared to 32 per cent positive, and in his third term his net disapproval rose to 33 percentage points. His successor, Gordon Brown, did little better; his net disapproval rating averaged 26 percentage points.

The net ratings of three Conservative prime ministers since 2010 have maintained the pattern of the dissatisfied outnumbering those satisfied. David Cameron had a negative rating of 10 percentage points when the Conservatives won the 2015 election, and it was similar when he lost the 2016 Brexit referendum and his office with it. Theresa May called a general election early in her time in office because she was approved by 56 per cent of the electorate. However, this lead was not translated into votes. May lost her majority at the 2017 election and averaged 34 per cent approval and 62 per cent disapproval before resigning under pressure from Conservative MPs.

Voters dissatisfied with the performance of the prime minister of the day may instead give approval to the leader of the Opposition. Since 1956 polls have collected data about satisfaction with 15 Conservative and Labour Opposition leaders. They include five who went on to become prime minister; seven who fought and never won an election; and three who never fought an election. The standard poll question parallels that about the prime minister: *Are you satisfied or dissatisfied with the way ... is doing his job as a Leader of the Opposition?*

Because the leader of the Opposition receives far less media attention than the prime minister, respondents with no opinion about them are more numerous than for the occupant of Downing Street. This reduces the satisfaction rating of the Opposition leader, especially in the months shortly after taking up their position. A skillful Opposition leader can benefit from this, since it is easier to win approval from those with no opinion than from those who disapprove. When Blair became leader of the Opposition in 1994 half the respondents had no opinion about him. By November 1995 the don't knows had shrunk to less than one-quarter of respondents and two-thirds of those who had newly formed an opinion endorsed Blair.

Opposition leaders have averaged an approval rating of 36 per cent.

Harold Wilson is the only Opposition leader who has sustained the approval of more than half the electorate during his first period in that post (Table 4.2). In addition, Hugh Gaitskell, Wilson in his second term, John Smith, Tony Blair and Keir Starmer have each been approved by an average of at least 45 per cent. David Cameron was rewarded for his efforts to 'de-toxify' the Conservative party by gaining the best Conservative approval rating, 39 per cent.

The Labour party has had three Opposition leaders—Michael Foot, Ed Miliband and Jeremy Corbyn—who have failed to average approval by as much as one-third of the electorate. All have been from the left of the party. Michael Foot turned in the poorest performance of any leader, satisfying an average of only one-sixth of the electorate. The first three leaders the Conservatives put up against Tony Blair—William Hague, Iain Duncan Smith and Michael Howard—had difficulty in securing the approval of as much as one-quarter of the electorate.

Table 4.2 Opposition leaders vary in popularity

	Low	Average (Per cent approving)	High
Gaitskell, Lab	32	46	57
Wilson, Lab	44	59	67
Heath, Con	24	34	51
Wilson, Lab	38	49	66
Thatcher, Con	31	41	64
Foot, Lab	9	17	38
Kinnock, Lab	26	38	58
J. Smith, Lab	43	46	53
Blair, Lab	33	46	53
Hague, Con	19	24	29
Duncan Smith, Con	16	22	27
Howard, Con	22	26	31
Cameron, Con	25	39	53
Miliband. Lab	21	31	41
Corbyn, Lab	15	29	44
Starmer, Lab	38	45	51

Sources As in Table 4.1

Nine Opposition leaders from Hugh Gaitskell in the late 1950s to Keir Starmer have been endorsed by more than half the electorate for at least one month (Table 4.2). Harold Wilson had ratings as high as 67 per cent in 1963 in the dying days of a Conservative government. The Gallup Poll gave Margaret Thatcher a rating as high as 64 per cent approval immediately after she replaced a discredited Ted Heath; this was 11 points higher than her peak result when in Downing Street. Michael Foot had his satisfaction rating fall to 9 per cent after losing the 1983 election, and Jeremy Corbyn's rating was as low as 15 per cent in the run-up to the 2019 general election. Opposition leaders are divided between those who see their approval rating increase, a harbinger of winning an election, and those who either see it decrease or are caught in a low-level equilibrium trap and see their vote changing little because they are going nowhere (Table 4.2).

Since the leader of the Opposition is the alternative prime minister, the system of political leadership is in good health if the leadership index, showing the combined approval of the two competitors for Downing Street, is close to 100 per cent. For this to happen it is not necessary for both the prime minister and the leader of the Opposition to be rated highly. When the prime minister is low in popular approval, a high level of approval for the leader of the Opposition can compensate. When the leader of the Opposition is unpopular, the collective rating will drop but this is only a problem for party government if the prime minister is unpopular too and the leadership index drops below two-thirds of the electorate.[1]

The fluctuations of the leadership index have been as much affected by the weakness of Opposition leaders of both parties as by the ups and downs in approval of the prime minister (Fig. 4.1). It went to 100 per cent when Harold Macmillan and Alec Douglas-Home faced popular Opposition leaders Hugh Gaitskell and Harold Wilson. It stayed that way with Heath and Callaghan in government and Thatcher in opposition. Since the 1979 Parliament the index has intermittently shown symptoms of bad health. It fell to 54 per cent, dragged down by Foot being the most unpopular Opposition leader on record and Thatcher being below average for prime ministership. The nomination of Neil Kinnock as Opposition

[1] The rating of the Liberal Democrats' leader is not included in these calculations since, however, popular they may be, no Liberal Democrat is a credible candidate for the prime ministership.

leader restored the health of the system for the next two Parliaments, only to be followed by fluctuations with the ups and downs of John Major's premiership.

Fluctuations have continued since Blair became Labour leader. Initially he pulled the index up as Opposition leader and in his first term as prime minister. However, his subsequent loss of popularity was not counterbalanced by the Conservative Opposition having a popular leader until after David Cameron was chosen in 2005. Since 2010 the leadership index has tended to be held up by three Conservative prime ministers while pushed down by the relative unpopularity of Ed Miliband and Jeremy Corbyn.

Popular attitudes towards party leaders are in democratic good health: their performance counts more than their personality. People critically judge Conservative and Labour leaders on the basis of the job they are doing and the party they lead. This accounts for the ups and downs of leaders' popularity during their term of office. A poorly performing prime minister is only a temporary problem as long as there is an acceptable leader of the Opposition waiting to take control of government at the next election. Two low points in the leadership index have occurred because of extremely low ratings for Opposition leaders, Foot and Corbyn. Twice both the prime minister and the Opposition leader have been very low in popularity; this occurred when Margaret Thatcher faced Michael Foot and Tony Blair faced Michael Howard.

4.4   Two Ways to Become an Ex-Prime Minister

Entering Downing Street is the highest step up the ladder of ambition for a British party leader, but it is not the final step. That takes place when a prime minister leaves office. Reward and punishment are complementary parts of democratic body politic. If a prime minister's government is viewed as performing well, the prime minister should win re-election. If the government is seen as performing badly, then the prime minister can be held accountable and removed from office by the governing party or by the electorate. Political ill health in Downing Street is thus a temporary problem for which changing prime ministers is the cure.

Winning re-election is necessary but not sufficient to ensure a long stay in Downing Street. At any time during the life of a Parliament, the governing party can formally or informally withdraw their support. In the Conservative party's 1922 Committee a letter signed by 15 per cent of

MPs is sufficient to trigger a vote of no confidence in their leader when he or she is prime minister. Even if a prime minister wins with the support of the payroll vote (that is, ministerial appointees), a substantial minority showing no confidence can be sufficient to force the leader's resignation. When Labour is in government, a vote of no confidence in the party's leader can occur only if it is demanded by 20 per cent of the party's MPs and a ballot is approved by the party's annual conference, which is dominated by the voice of trade unions and constituency parties.

By the standards of leaving office voluntarily, all but one prime minister since 1945 left office like King Charles I, with their stature significantly diminished. Harold Wilson was unique in leaving Downing Street voluntarily with the Labour party ahead of the Conservatives in the opinion polls. Wilson said that after 36 years on the firing line in Westminster and Whitehall he had run out of energy and was addressing old problems with old solutions. At the age of 60, Wilson retired to an easier and more profitable life as an elder statesman who had won four of the five general elections he fought. His long-time rival, Jim Callaghan, was left to deal with an economic crisis in the making.

By the standards of electoral success, Margaret Thatcher and Tony Blair are outstanding. Each won three successive elections, first as leader of the Opposition and the next two as the nation's prime minister. Thatcher's 11 years in office and Blair's 10 years make them the two longest-serving prime ministers since the late nineteenth century. Harold Macmillan and Anthony Eden each had an unspoiled record, winning the one election they fought after entering Downing Street while the Conservatives were in power.

The importance of the prime minister's performance as a government leader is shown when a party leader sometimes wins and sometimes loses elections. Six prime ministers have done both. Clement Attlee won two elections by defeating Winston Churchill, who then ousted Attlee from Downing Street in 1951. Harold Wilson won the first two elections he fought, but then was rejected on the basis of the government's performance during six years in office. Ted Heath took office from Wilson, but was rejected in two 1974 elections when the electorate voted Wilson back into office. John Major fought two elections, winning the first in 1992 but, after the government was divided by Europe and weakened by the fall in the pound, losing the second. David Cameron won his first two elections as party leader, only to resign immediately after losing the 2016 Brexit referendum.

MPs threatened with losing their seat if their leader loses Downing Street have an incentive to try to change their personal fortune by changing their party leader. Conservative prime ministers have more often left office under pressure from their own MPs than by being rejected by the electorate. Because MPs see the prime minister at close hand in the House of Commons, they can spot signs of physical ill health. After much resistance, the 81-year-old Winston Churchill was persuaded to retire with dignity rather than have his frailties exposed by a general election campaign. Anthony Eden's mishandling of the Suez War severely aggravated a chronic medical condition, making him unfit to retain office. The Conservatives were 16 percentage points behind Labour when Harold Macmillan was hospitalized with what appeared to be a serious medical problem. This gave him a diplomatic excuse to resign with dignity before insecure MPs publicly ousted him.

Three prime ministers were told to go by their Cabinet colleagues and MPs responsible for liaising with backbench MPs. When Thatcher was challenged to a vote of no confidence, she fell just short of the super-majority required to win the first-round ballot and was threatened with losing the second round by the entry of more popular senior colleagues. Thanks to the payroll vote of MPs holding government appointments, Theresa May won her first vote of confidence among Tory MPs, even though 117 Conservatives voted no confidence. With her Brexit policy in shreds, she resigned five months later when a second vote of confidence was imminent. When Blair was in 10 Downing Street there was continuing fighting with 'Planet f—', his staff's name for the next-door office of the Chancellor of the Exchequer, Gordon Brown. After Blair won his third election victory in 2005, Brown actively began campaigning for Blair to deliver on his promise to leave office rather than fight a fourth election. With Labour trailing the Conservatives in the opinion polls for 11 consecutive months, Blair let Brown have the office Brown longed for.

The electorate can hold the governing party accountable for its choice of a prime minister in the middle of a Parliament and reject its choice at the next election. Sir Alec Douglas-Home was a compromise choice because, unlike the three front-runners, he had no enemies in the House of Commons, having long been a hereditary member of the House of Lords. Jim Callaghan beat Michael Foot by a four-to-three majority because Labour MPs considered that Callaghan's formidable ministerial experience made him more qualified to head a government than Foot's oratorical ability. No senior Labour MP wanted to challenge

Gordon Brown, the determined and self-appointed heir apparent, for the succession to Tony Blair. None of the three survived their first electoral test.

The British system of choosing and replacing candidates for the prime ministership is usually in good political health. It ensures that a would-be prime minister is scrutinized for years within the party before being chosen as party leader. If the Opposition chooses a candidate because of their narrow ideological appeal to party members, the electorate can reject their choice and the Opposition will have to make a different choice if it wants to gain control of the government. There is no election law that limits a popular prime minister to two terms in office as in the United States. Nor does a prime minister have the job security of a fixed-term American president. Instead, a prime minister who loses the confidence of their party can be abruptly ejected from Downing Street by a vote of no confidence by the party's MPs, and the electorate subsequently has the power to confirm or reject the party's choice at the next general election.

REFERENCES

Kempsell, Ross. 2020. Ministers to Miss Out on Party Piece. *The Times*, September 7.

King, Anthony, and R.J. Wybrow. 2001. *British Political Opinion 1937–2000: The Gallup Polls*. London: Politico's.

Newton, Kenneth. 2020. Government Communications, Political Trust and Compliant Social Behaviour. *Political Quarterly* 91 (3): 502–513.

Parker, George, and Sebastian Payne. 2020. Brexit and Virus Blunders Leave Johnson Reeling. *Financial Times*, September 19.

Rose, Richard. 1995. A Crisis of Confidence in British Party Leaders? *Contemporary Record* 9 (2): 273–293.

Rose, Richard. 2001. *The Prime Minister in a Shrinking World*. Oxford and Boston: Polity Press.

Shipman, Tim. 2020. Anxious Johnson Seeks a Makeover. *The Sunday Times*, October 11.

Thatcher, Margaret. 1993. *The Downing Street Years*. London: HarperCollins.

Weber, Max. 1958. *From Max Weber: Essays in Sociology*. New York: Oxford University Press.

CHAPTER 5

Whitehall's Collective Brainpower

The body politic is a singular entity, while government is a collective noun that encompasses the many departments found in Whitehall and its environs. Each department has particular policy responsibilities; collectively, they have far more staff and brainpower than Downing Street. Because responsibility for policy is clearly fixed on the party in power, departmental ministers are collectively accountable to the electorate. This avoids the confusion that exists in Washington, where departmental secretaries are accountable to the White House and to Congressional committees that supervise them.

The democratic direction of government requires both political legitimacy and knowledge of how government works. Because ministers are elected, they have the legitimacy to decide what the government ought to do. They also have special expertise in what the French call *la politique politicienne*, the politics of politicians, campaigning for support for themselves and their activities in the electorate, in their party and among their fellow Cabinet ministers. However, expertise in political campaigning does not give politicians knowledge of how Whitehall works.

Ministers need help if what they promise is to become an effective public policy. As permanent employees of government, civil servants have the expertise needed to turn a minister's expression of will into a policy that can be piloted through Whitehall and Parliament. Because they must

© The Author(s), under exclusive license to Springer Nature
Switzerland AG 2021
R. Rose, *How Sick Is British Democracy?*
Challenges to Democracy in the 21st Century,
https://doi.org/10.1007/978-3-030-73123-6_5

serve both Conservative and Labour ministers, civil servants claim to be apolitical. In fact, they are bisexual, taking a position in keeping with the political demands of their minister of the moment. Civil servants are skilled in exercising 'won't power' when they view a minister's will as violating Whitehall's first rule: politics is the art of the possible. They can respond to a ministerial direction in language that appears to show agreement. However, phrases such as 'Up to a point, minister' or 'Is that wise, minister?' are veiled warnings that doing what their minister wants could end in political grief.

Traditionally, ministers and civil servants pooled their brains to formulate policies in the privacy of Whitehall. Ministers could set out broad policy guidelines and make major decisions on political issues, while senior civil servants practised what German sociologist Max Weber (1958) preached: 'Power is above all the administration of everyday things'. Their co-operation upheld the doctrine of ministerial accountability to Parliament while giving senior civil servants the professional satisfaction of making use of their knowledge and experience of how Whitehall works. The relationship between ministers and civil servants was one of mutual respect. Critics called it a system of making public policy in private.

Margaret Thatcher changed the relationship between politicians and civil servants to meet her conception of democratic party government: elected politicians had the right not only to make policies but also to be served by people who would deliver what ministers wanted. Instead of civil servants canvassing alternative policy options and the objections to each, Thatcher wanted 'can do' officials who would use their knowledge to help achieve the government's goals. She singled out as her ideal a businessman, Lord Young of Graffham, whom she brought into Whitehall to advise on privatizing nationalized industries. Thatcher contrasted those who brought her problems with Lord Young, who brought her solutions. Ministers and civil servants who did not adopt a 'can do' attitude towards her agenda were sidelined.

Tony Blair began turning Whitehall into an open market for policy-making. He brought in two outsiders as chief advisers with the power to give orders to civil servants. Blair's practice of formulating policies through discussions with trusted personal staff sitting on sofas often excluded civil servants. Boris Johnson entered Downing Street with a single-issue programme—Get Brexit done—that required political skills rather than Whitehall knowledge. To achieve this goal, he turned to

Dominic Cummings, a key strategist in campaigning for Brexit. Unusually among campaigners, Cummings also had a strong policy agenda. Johnson's dislike of engaging in detailed policymaking gave Cummings substantial scope for advancing policies. Cummings participated in meetings about Treasury policy, defence and handling coronavirus until the way he exercised his borrowed power created so much controversy that Johnson terminated Cummings' appointment in November 2020 and Cummings struck back by telling MPs of Johnson's faults.

Democratic government is in good health when Whitehall's collective brainpower produces policies that reflect the objectives of the governing party. This requires Cabinet ministers with the skills needed to give direction to large Whitehall departments and enough time in charge of a department to come to grips with the policies and problems for which they are accountable. Democratic policymaking requires openness to advisers with knowledge relevant to the particular problem a minister faces. It is healthy when the experience of civil servants is augmented by the expertise of outside advisers. Democratic accountability is in good health when the governing party takes responsibility for all its policies. It is in bad health if ministers try to shuffle out of responsibility when things go wrong by being economical with the truth or dumping blame on their civil servants.

5.1   CABINET MINISTERS FILL
GAPS LEFT BY DOWNING STREET

Decisions made in Downing Street can only be implemented by ministers and civil servants in departments with the authority to take action. For example, military force is managed by the Ministry of Defence, public spending by the Treasury, and health care by public sector institutions accountable to multiple ministers. Collectively, Cabinet ministers have institutional and staff resources that Downing Street lacks. Circular reasoning may dismiss the activities of Cabinet ministers and their departments as of little importance because they are not in the hands of Downing Street. However, it is a sophist fallacy to assume that a lot of little decisions do not have a big collective impact on what government does.

Whitehall departments vary greatly in what they do and in their political importance. The Departments of the Treasury, Business, Trade and Transport are responsible for policies that influence the economy and thereby affect electoral support. The Departments of Health and Social Care, Work and Pensions, Education, and Culture and Sport deal with social affairs that affect the lives of most voters. Immigration, crime and the law are of prime concern to the Home Office, the Department of Justice and the Attorney General's Office. Local and regional conditions are in the hands of Departments for Housing and Local Government, the Environment, Scotland, Wales and Northern Ireland. The Foreign, Commonwealth and Development Office and the Ministry of Defence focus on the world far beyond Westminster.

Every department is a conglomerate of sub-departments and dependent public sector institutions. For example, the secretary of state for the Department for Business, Energy and Industrial Strategy is responsible for 41 agencies affiliated to the department. He also represents the department to other Cabinet ministers, to Parliament, to the media and to interest groups. During the coronavirus crisis, the secretary of state provided the reassurance to businesses concerned about government policies on the pandemic. He is caught in the middle between businesses wanting to know about Brexit policies and Number 10, where these policies are determined. In his activities the secretary of state is supported by six ministers of state and parliamentary under-secretaries dealing with specific departmental responsibilities on his behalf. Given the many responsibilities of Cabinet ministers, more than five-sixths of the decisions about delegated rules and regulations for which they are nominally responsible are prepared by civil servants and signed off by subordinate ministers who try to imagine what the minister would regard as acceptable (Page 2001: 88).

The minister's job. Individual ministers have two linked priorities: boosting their own political careers and dealing with departmental responsibilities. As temporary officeholders, ministers give priority to what they can do to promote fresh policies that will enhance their personal reputation in the limited time they are there. They can deal with their responsibility to make decisions in a variety of ways. The party manifesto usually contains multiple policy commitments for each department, and civil servants are at hand to provide details of how commitments can be implemented. If the commitment has no obvious or attractive solution, a minister can try to avoid taking any decision. If a decision involves competing goods, such as spending a limited budget increase on primary schools, on secondary education or on higher education, then a minister must use his or her personal judgement. Events, whether desirable such as an automatic increase in pensions or undesirable such as an unexpected rise in poverty among pensioners, demand a response from the minister.

The circumstances are limited in which a minister can initiate a policy as his or her own. Every minister inherits a large portfolio of departmental policies introduced and amended by Conservative and Labour predecessors. The legacy includes laws that limit what the minister can do, spending commitments that leave little money to fund new initiatives, and formal and informal departmental norms and practices that are not easily altered by a transient Cabinet minister. This legacy of past commitments limits what a minister can do.

Ambitious Cabinet ministers welcome being the department's public face, promoting its policies and, incidentally, themselves to media audiences. The minister for education can announce he or she has decided to build more than 100 new schools when the money comes from the Treasury, and the schools are built by the private sector and operated by local authorities. The flip side is that when a department experiences an unwelcome event, such as the collapse of a bridge, the minister must explain why he or she hadn't prevented what was the consequence of negligence by predecessors of both parties.

It is a win-win outcome when a minister can boost both their career and the standing of their department by being responsible for a popular major policy. As the minister of Health, Housing and Local Government in the 1945–1951 Labour government, Aneurin Bevan achieved a lasting reputation for himself and the Labour government by being in charge of the National Health Service Act of 1946. Inadvertently, Bevan contributed to the reputation of his Conservative successor as housing minister, for Harold Macmillan was able to take credit for increasing by half the number of houses built annually when Bevan was in charge.

The link between departmental policy and a minister's reputation can sometimes produce a lose-lose outcome, as happened to Norman Lamont. By the time he became Chancellor of the Exchequer in 1990, Lamont was regarded as a potential prime minister. However, he also inherited from his predecessor, John Major, responsibility for the British pound being tied to the European Exchange Rate Mechanism at a rate that was vulnerable to speculation. In September 1992 Lamont tried and failed to save the pound's value from falling by raising the bank rate from 5 to 15 per cent in one day. The pound's exchange rate crashed and with it Lamont's reputation. When he offered to resign, Prime Minister John

Major refused to accept it, keeping Lamont in place as a shield protecting Major from criticism.

A lucky politician can become a political success if their failure is overlooked. When Theresa May became head of the Home Office in 2010, she announced that it would reduce net immigration to fewer than 100,000 a year and introduced a policy to discourage immigrants from coming to Britain. In the same month in which David Cameron resigned as prime minister, official figures showed that net immigration had risen to 332,000 a year, the highest in a quarter of a century (https://mig rationobservatory.ox.ac.uk/). The following month May became prime minister.

Shuffling and reshuffling ministers. The prime minister of a newly elected government must make up to 100 ministerial appointments. Being a minister requires the ability to manage a large and complex department as well as the House of Commons. As the work of Whitehall has grown, there are fewer sinecures that MPs who lack ministerial competence can be given as a reward for their loyalty to the prime minister. Most departments have five or six junior ministers supporting the secretary of state in charge of the department; the Home Office and the Foreign, Commonwealth and Development Office each have eight ministers. Unlike many parliamentary democracies where Cabinet ministers can be chosen from a national pool, British ministers must be Members of Parliament. A substantial fraction of the governing party's MPs are not suited to be offered posts; they are inexperienced newcomers, unsuitable on political grounds or because of personal failings, or uninterested in taking on the burdens of ministerial office. While the prime minister has the discretion to decide which office and which rank ministers have, there is a very restricted choice in the people who are given those 100 ministerial posts.

Appointing ministers is not a management selection process in which the skills required to head a particular department are first identified and individuals then matched to a job for which they are qualified. Instead, the prime minister makes up a Cabinet by selecting people who will be loyal from conviction, calculation, hope of further preferment or fear of dismissal if they oppose him or her. The prime minister uses patronage as the glue to hold together a governing party whose MPs have diverse views, abilities and ambitions. Theresa May appointed Cabinet ministers with opposing views about Brexit in the hope that the convention of collective Cabinet responsibility would force them to back whatever

Brexit policy she followed. This did not happen; more than three dozen ministers resigned because of disagreement.

A healthy government requires Cabinet ministers who are not only skilled in the politics of party and Parliament but also experienced in the practices of Whitehall. Knowledge is needed of how policy goals can be converted into Acts of Parliament setting out the administrative means by which policies can be delivered to their intended beneficiaries. Being a journalist, a teacher or a political assistant to an MP does not provide that experience. Jacqui Smith (2009), an Oxford PPE graduate appointed home secretary by Gordon Brown, confessed: 'When I became Home Secretary, I'd never run a major organisation. I hope I did a good job. But if I did, it was more by luck than by any kind of development of skills. I think we should have been better trained. I think there should have been more induction'.

When a new government takes office after more than a decade in opposition, it cannot be staffed by experienced ministers. Tony Blair formed his first Cabinet after Labour had been in opposition for 18 years. Meanwhile, a whole generation of former Labour ministers had retired. The great majority of ministerial posts went to Labour MPs who were as new to government office as Blair was. When David Cameron became prime minister of a Conservative–Liberal Democrat coalition government in 2010, his party had been out of office for 13 years, and the Liberal party had not been in government since long before most Liberal MPs were born. Cameron, Deputy Prime Minister Nick Clegg, the Chancellor of the Exchequer and the Home Secretary were all novices in government.

While ministers in a newly elected government are fresh in office, their departments are steeped in past commitments. In the mordant words of a Conservative chancellor handing over to a new Labour minister, 'You inherit our problems and our solutions'. Civil servants will have ready a memorandum about how the manifesto pledges of the winning party can be implemented, if only up to a point. When a new minister arrives midway in the life of a Parliament, he or she will be given detailed briefings about the state of play left behind by the departing minister, including ticking time-bombs. The legacy can be worse for a newly elected government. When Joel Barnett, a Labour Treasury minister, told me in early 1979 how bad the government's finance would be for his Conservative successor, I said, 'You mean the cupboard is bare?' His answer was: 'Worse than that; we burnt the shelves!'

When a governing party has been re-elected for a second or third term, there is a big supply of MPs who have shown what they can and can't do in government. Brown and May could and did form Cabinets of experienced ministers. The 'fresh' face of government that the media heralded was not fresh to civil servants. Exceptionally, after winning the December 2019 election, Johnson felt confident enough of controlling his party to exclude from office experienced ministers whose loyalty to himself was in doubt. Instead of making Cabinet appointments that compensated for his own lack of experience and interest in Whitehall processes, Johnson appointed 17 Cabinet ministers who had never been in charge of a department before.

During the life of a Parliament, the prime minister makes changes in the government's ministerial team, as ministers who cause problems are pushed out and a few resign in disagreement with a government policy. When a minister makes a major mistake, there is an inclination to accept the minister's account of what happened rather than accept blame that implicates the government as a whole. However, if there is sufficient disquiet among the party's MPs along with opinion poll evidence that the minister is a political liability, then they can be given the choice of resigning or being sacked.

Major reshuffles are often an attempt by prime ministers to boost their sagging popularity. For example, after the Labour government suffered a bad setback at local government elections in 2006, Tony Blair changed the ministers in charge of Whitehall departments unconcerned with local government such as the Foreign Office, Defence and the Home Office with the intention of putting a new face on his government. Blair's approval rating sagged lower still.

It is unhealthy for democratic accountability if ministers are reshuffled so often that they do not have enough time to gain substantive knowledge of all the policies for which they are responsible. It can take a year for a new minister to learn what his or her department is doing, for better or for worse, and another year or more to prepare new policies and alter inherited policies. The prime minister's practice of reshuffling Cabinet posts during the life of a Parliament reduces the time that a minister has to learn about their department and make effective policies. Ministers who expect to be moved about frequently can boost their career by concentrating on immediately visible activities rather than long-term goals. In the quarter-century since Blair became prime minister there have been seven elections and four changes of prime minister, each the occasion for a Cabinet reshuffle, plus reshuffles during each Parliament.

The average tenure of the secretary of state in charge of a major government department is just over two and one-half years. Thus, each Whitehall department can expect to have at least two ministers in charge during a single Parliament. The Home Office, the Foreign Office, Health, Education and Defence have each had ten chief ministers since 1997. The Treasury is different, since Blair kept Brown as Chancellor for ten years because the only other post that Brown would accept was Blair's job as prime minister. Since Brown left, turnover at the Treasury has reverted to normal; there have been five chancellors in 13 years. There is no significant difference in the turnover rate between Conservative and Labour governments or between departments.

Government by Cabinet ministers has a recurring problem of health. When a newly elected government has the most political legitimacy to introduce new policies developed in opposition, it is likely to have many ministers who have no experience of being a Cabinet minister. When a party controls the government for two or more consecutive Parliaments, there will be a number of experienced ministers but fewer fresh ideas. The likelihood of having a short time in charge of a department is an incentive for ministers to give priority to announcing popular policy intentions, such as upgrading vocational education, without being able to deliver an ambitious promise. The Cabinet minister for business can take headline credit for committing Britain to a net zero level of greenhouse gas emissions in 2050, knowing that he or she will be long gone from office before it is clear whether what works as a political tactic has also worked as a government policy.

5.2 Opening up the Market for Policymaking

Re-organizing Whitehall departments is the traditional public administration prescription for stimulating a fresh approach to policymaking. It is easy to apply in Whitehall, because the functions of departments are not fixed by an Act of Parliament; the prime minister has the discretion to re-allocate responsibilities between departments. Renaming a department without changing what goes on within it is particularly attractive as a means of putting a fresh face on government with minimal change in the functioning of the body politic (see Davies and Rose 1988).

Re-organizing Whitehall activities to make a single minister responsible for co-ordinating policy conflicts does not deal with the causes of the conflict. The merger of five different departments concerned with military defence simply made inter-departmental conflicts intra-departmental conflicts. It did not get rid of disputes about whether threats to the country's security are best dealt with by soldiers' boots on the ground, aircraft in the sky, nuclear submarines or computer specialists in new forms of cyber-warfare. The secretary of state for Defence must still decide which programmes benefit and which are cut when allocating limited funds for national defence.

Opening up Whitehall departments to outsiders began in mid-Victorian times when industrialization and urbanization created fresh problems that gentlemanly officials and patronage appointees could not cope with. The post of Chief Medical Officer was created in 1865. In the Second World War specialists in operations research formulated strategies to evade submarine threats, and economists and market researchers advised about allocating resources for war production and for food rationing. The Government Economic Service was founded in 1964 and the Government Statistical Service in 1968.

As the scope of public policy affected more and more parts of society, interest groups began to liaise with the Whitehall departments in charge of policies affecting their members' activities. The Trades Union Congress was founded in 1868 and the National Farmers Union in 1908. Interest groups seek to influence policies by offering Whitehall officials information and advice about drafting policies to their benefit. When the government of the day is committed to a policy imposing costs on the group's members, interest groups seek mitigation of its effects in return for not engaging in a public campaign against the government and co-operating in implementing policies.

The use of experts who are known supporters of the governing party began to take root when Harold Wilson was prime minister. He brought into government as short-term advisers internationally known economists and social policy professors who were also well-known Fabian socialists. Similarly, Ted Heath and Margaret Thatcher turned to business people who shared their views on the value of government following good business practice.

Special advisers (spads) give political support to their minister that senior civil servants are neither expected nor qualified to offer since they have not been party activists. Spads support their minister's political reputation in the media and in the governing party. As temporary political civil servants, spads have access to confidential documents circulated to their minister and participate in departmental meetings as well as informal discussions with their minister. They can push for the inclusion of symbolic phrases or substantive measures that may gain popularity for their minister and oppose departmental proposals that would generate unfavourable publicity and opposition from the governing party's MPs. Although spads have no formal authority, their closeness to a minister makes their views influential. The total number of spads in Whitehall departments is upwards of 100.

The prime minister can have a team of spads to monitor activities in Whitehall departments that may affect his or her political reputation. They can thus compensate for the limited time that the prime minister has to keep track of what the various limbs of government are doing and to avoid being caught off guard by a department advancing a policy that is unwelcome in Downing Street. Although the prime minister's spads have no standing within the departments of ministers, their position means that their questions and suggestions cannot be ignored by departmental civil servants who do not know to what extent a particular spad's views represent those of the spad's minister.

British think tanks have entered the market for policymaking by promoting political principles and policies free of the constraints of civil servants bound to the principles of the government of the day and of political parties giving priority to electioneering. Think tanks usually focus on a particular field of public policy, be it economic affairs, national security or immigration. They have a small staff and a network of experts preparing reports that advocate policies going beyond the position of the government of the day. Their views tend to be more in harmony with either the Conservatives, for example, the Institute of Economic Affairs, or Labour, such as the Institute for Public Policy Research. Some think tanks, such as the Institute for Fiscal Studies, take policy positions that are relevant to both parties, but not consistently aligned with either. Demand for their ideas is high when the party a think tank is aligned with is in opposition. When the party is in government, think tanks have the bittersweet reward of seeing their staff depleted by recruitment into government as spads and friendly MPs no longer needing their support because they have become Whitehall ministers.

The reduction in the size of civil service has enabled consulting firms such as McKinsey & Company to profit from Whitehall departments commissioning their assistance in devising and implementing public policies. Advice can come from people experienced in advising private sector clients. Both Conservative and Labour governments have turned to management consultants to advise on policies. The EU Exit Unit in the Cabinet Office spent £130 million on media and public relations consultants to promote an understanding of what Brexit required and since Brexit became final has spent £180 million with six management consultancy firms to advise on immigration, international trade, and food and health care supplies.

The coronavirus pandemic gives a very public demonstration of the relevance to policy of the knowledge of public health experts, scientists, statisticians and economists. Their diagnoses usually conclude with statements about the probability of the virus spreading if the government does nothing and that any policy chosen has both costs and benefits. A 'stay home' policy to protect health has costs for the economy, while maintaining normal activities before the virus can be controlled risks a rising death rate. The choice between policies increasing costs to human life or to the economy cannot be decided by science. It is a political decision that must be made by the prime minister after receiving competing views from ministers and experts.

The market for policymaking in Westminster today is no longer a hierarchy in which the minister is on top and civil servants under them. It is a bazaar in which a wide variety of people and organizations with political views congenial to the government of the day can participate. Experienced civil servants are included but their number has been depleted by government cuts and competition for their talent from other well-paying careers.

The opening up of Whitehall departments to a variety of advisers to ministers has been good for the mental health of British democracy because public policymaking is no longer the private activity of a small number of people. In an age in which people communicate by emails that can be readily retrieved and official documents can readily be copied it is harder to maintain official secrecy. There is an open market in which think tanks, consultants and academic experts offer ideas and evidence to Whitehall departments, committees in the House of Commons and the media. Ministers no longer need to rely exclusively on civil servants for advice; they are continuously exposed to advice from people with independent expertise about their department's work and political advisers who can support their political work and careers.

The variety of policy sources puts a strain on democratic accountability because most advisers are not elected. Some have an authority based on professional recognition or business success, while others are politically trusted confidantes of their minister. Outsiders such as Alastair Campbell, Tony Blair's media supremo, did not want to be democratically accountable to Parliament. He was satisfied with being accountable to the prime minister.

5.3   SHUFFLING AND RESHUFFLING ACCOUNTABILITY

For generations ministers and Whitehall civil servants have paid lip service to democratic accountability by engaging in a charade. Cabinet ministers took full political responsibility for what their department was doing. However little they may have contributed to the formulation of a new measure, they introduced it to Parliament with the words, 'I have decided'. Civil servants cloaked their authority in the phrase 'The Secretary of State has directed that', when the minister may have had no interest in what the official was doing. Published documents could be written in a mandarin code that required translation to have its meaning known, for example, describing a bad decision as one that could be improved (Mackenzie 1969). The minister got the public credit for the department's achievements and civil servants got the private satisfaction of a job well done.

Whitehall maintains the doctrine that, if a departmental policy comes unstuck, the current minister is expected to give an account of what went wrong. Being accountable is not the same as being personally responsible and therefore culpable. Many failings revealed by unexpected and unwanted events are the cumulative consequence of decisions taken over decades by ministers of both parties and civil servants. For example, Grenfell Tower, where a fire killed 72 residents in June 2017, was designed in keeping with Ministry of Housing standards set in 1961. Plans were approved by the local council in 1970; the high-rise block was completed by private contractors in 1974, and then managed by a private sector agency. The local tenants' group began reporting safety defects and fire risks several years prior to renovation begun by private contractors in 2015.

When there is a major failing that the government does not want to try to defend, it can authorize a formal inquiry to produce an after-the-fact explanation of what went wrong. While inquiries are nominally described as independent, the government sets the terms of reference specifying what the inquiry should look into and what it should turn a blind eye to. Inquiries are expected to move slowly so that by the time the report is issued its findings will only be of historical interest. The day after the Grenfell Tower fire, Prime Minister Theresa May announced there would be a formal inquiry led by a retired judge with terms of reference shielding ministers and civil servants. The inquiry was directed to focus on the immediate causes of the fire and how it was fought. The head of the Fire Brigades Union and independent academics criticized the terms for ignoring the extent to which the Ministry of Housing regulations and lax enforcement contributed to the disaster.

If the government of the day has to give a public account in defence of an unsuccessful policy, the informal Whitehall guidelines are: don't tell lies but be selective when telling the truth. The classic exposition of this practice was given by the head of the civil service, Sir Robert Armstrong (1986), when questioned under oath in an unsuccessful government action to prevent the publication of a book about British spying.

Q: So that letter contains a lie, does it not?

Armstrong: It contains a misleading impression in that respect.

Q: Which you knew to be misleading at the time you made it?

Armstrong: Of course.

Q: So it contains a lie?

Armstrong: It is a misleading impression, it does not contain a lie, I don't think.

Q: What is the difference between a misleading impression and a lie?

Armstrong: You are as good at English as I am.

Q: I am just trying to understand.

Armstrong: A lie is a straight untruth.

Q: What is a misleading impression – a sort of bent untruth?

Armstrong: As one person said, it is perhaps being economical with the truth.

The ministerial practice of being economical with the truth imposes a cost on democratic health by creating popular disbelief in politicians. When Ipsos MORI (2019) asked whether people in 25 different professions could be trusted to tell the truth, politicians and government ministers were close to the bottom. Only 14 per cent trusted politicians to tell the truth and 17 per cent trusted government ministers. Both rated significantly below journalists, 26 per cent, in honesty. Distrust of politicians does not reflect widespread cynicism about the institutions of British society; 15 professions are trusted by more than half of British people.

The growth in the number of policies for which Whitehall ministers are directly or indirectly accountable has put pressure on ministers to defend departmental mistakes for which they were not culpable as well as those that were their fault. The minister in charge of the Home Office is particularly subject to stress because thousands of actions are taken by low-ranking officials who can make mistakes for which the minister is accountable. When that happens, the Home Secretary may put the blame on other public officials. When the Prison Service repeatedly showed faults in managing prisons, Conservative home secretary Michael Howard blamed the director general of the service even though the Home Office was an accessory before the fact for many of its problems. A Labour successor as home secretary, John Reid, told the House of Commons Home Affairs Select Committee, 'It's not my job to manage this department'. He described many parts of his department as 'dysfunctional'. Conservative home secretary Priti Patel has repeatedly told her civil servants that they are 'f—— useless' when they don't give her the advice she wants.

Since Boris Johnson established his political authority with a big election victory, Downing Street has turned the post of permanent secretary, the highest civil service post in a Whitehall department, into that of semi-permanent secretary with briefings describing them as 'unhelpful'. In less than nine months, permanent secretaries at the Foreign Office, the Home Office, Justice and Education have been pushed out, as has Mark Sedwill, the Cabinet Secretary and chief civil service adviser to the prime minister. When Gavin Williamson, the education minister and a Johnson supporter, did a U-turn after a public outcry about his handling of coronavirus-impacted examination results, he remained in place. The permanent secretary in the Education Department was ousted with less than a week's notice.

When the independent adviser on ministerial standards, Sir Alex Allan, found that Patel's bullying of senior civil servants had broken the ministerial code of behaviour, Johnson backed her, and Allan resigned. After an advertisement invited applications for the post of Sedwill's successor, a journalist reported that most of the likely candidates showed no interest in what they described as a job that was 'on a hiding to nothing' in a 'dysfunctional Downing Street' (Wright 2020).

The ministerial shuffling of blame on to civil servants has encouraged civil servants to emulate the practice of MPs and Cabinet ministers and leak documents to the media. The efforts of the government of the day to stop the practice are ineffective: a Google search of 'leaks UK government' produces more than 10 million results. In the House of Lords and letters to *The Times* recently retired senior civil servants voice criticisms of ministerial behaviour shared by their former colleagues still in Whitehall. The head of the First Division Association, the senior civil servants' trade union, has declared, 'It's clear that this government views civil servants as scapegoats, political pawns there only to help shield ministers from accountability' (Swinford 2020).

The policymaking process in Whitehall today shows multiple symptoms of democratic ill health. Many Cabinet ministers share a common infirmity: they lack experience in the management of large and complex organizations. This infirmity is increased by frequent reshuffles between posts limiting their time to learn what their department does. This creates incentives for ministers to focus on short-term measures that will boost their political standing rather than patiently engaging in crafting policies of long-term benefit. If a prime minister makes a minister's loyalty to Number 10 rather than competence the primary standard for holding their job, this frustrates Parliament's attempt to hold an inadequate minister to account.

The proliferation of policy advice available to ministers is a sign of good health but it has reduced democratic accountability. Because advisers are not MPs, they are not subject to questioning in the House of Commons about the advice that they give. Moreover, prime ministers on whom advisers depend for their influence have reduced the time for Parliament to hold them to account. Margaret Thatcher and John Major answered questions in the House of Commons twice a week, but Tony Blair switched to answering once a week, and his successors have maintained this practice. New policies are often announced first in the media instead of being presented first to Parliament, where MPs of all parties can ask pointed questions. The Speaker of the House of Commons, Sir Lindsay Hoyle, has publicly complained of the prime minister's lack of respect, reminding Downing Street (Maguire 2020): 'We don't have a president; we have a prime minister who is answerable to parliament.'

References

Armstrong, Sir Robert. 1986. https://en.wikipedia.org/wiki/Economical_with_ the_truth.

Davies, Phillip L., and Richard Rose. 1988. Are Programme Resources Related to Organizational Change? *European Journal of Political Research* 6: 73–98.

Ipsos MORI. 2019. *Veracity Index 2019: Trust in Professions Survey*. London: Ipsos MORI.

Mackenzie, W.J.M. 1969. The Plowden Report: A Translation. In *Policy-Making in Britain: A Reader in Government*, ed. R. Rose, 273–282. New York: St. Martins.

Maguire, Patrick. 2020. "Presidential PM" Sidelines Parliament. *The Times*, July 21.

Page, Edward C. 2001. *Governing by Numbers*. Oxford: Hart.

Smith, Jacqui. 2009. https://en.wikipedia.org/wiki/Jacqui_Smith. Retrieved 26 May 2020.

Swinford, Steven. 2020. No. 10 Forces out Top Schools Mandarin After Exams Fiasco. *The Times*, August 7.

Weber, Max. 1958. *From Max Weber: Essays in Sociology*. New York: Oxford University Press.

Wright, Oliver. 2020. Contenders to Lead Civil Service Tell No. 10: Thanks but No Thanks. *The Times*, August 7.

CHAPTER 6

The Limbs of a Disunited Kingdom

The full title of the United Kingdom of Great Britain and Northern Ireland is a reminder that the government of the United Kingdom is not an integrated nation-state but a multinational kingdom. Soldiers, judges and other public officials swear an oath of allegiance not to the British state but to the Queen. The passport of citizens of the United Kingdom is described on the cover as a British passport. The absence of a reference to England, the most populous part of the United Kingdom, does not mean that it is absent from the government of the United Kingdom. A Google search finds that the number of references to the English government is double those to the British government. There are also more than double the number of references to the Queen of England than to the Queen of Great Britain.

Since it was created in 1801 the United Kingdom has always been a multinational state. This fact was rarely mentioned until the late 1960s, when I started using the term in research on the non-English parts of the United Kingdom (Rose 1971: Chapter 2; Aughey 2018). The national flag, the Union Jack, combines the symbols of three nations, the St George's Cross of England, the St. Andrew's Cross of Scotland and the St. Patrick's Cross of Ireland. Wales is not represented in the Union Jack and historically legislation covering England has applied to Wales.

© The Author(s), under exclusive license to Springer Nature
Switzerland AG 2021
R. Rose, *How Sick Is British Democracy?*
Challenges to Democracy in the 21st Century,
https://doi.org/10.1007/978-3-030-73123-6_6

The use of the word British as the adjectival form of United Kingdom is a reminder that, unlike Americans, French, Germans and Italians, people do not identify themselves as Ukish. Unlike Ireland, the United Kingdom was not created by a national revolution in which identity came before the state was formed. Unlike Austria, which became a state after the break-up of the Habsburg Empire, the dissolution of the British Empire did not cause the break-up of the United Kingdom. Nor has political revolution led to the creation of a nation-building state, as occurred when 13 formerly British colonies became the United States of America. After King James VI of Scotland inherited the title of King of England in 1603, he attempted to popularize a single British identity for his dual monarchy. Scotland became North Britain and England was called South Britain. While the former term was in use in Scotland for several centuries, the term South Britain never caught on in England.

The boundaries of the United Kingdom are fixed by political history, not geography. It is not an island state but a Crown with shifting boundaries. For more than 800 years there has been a Kingdom of England. Great Britain was created by the union of the English and Scottish Kingdoms in 1707. A two-island United Kingdom was created when the Parliament of Ireland, for centuries a domain of the Crown, was absorbed into the British Parliament in 1801. Queen Victoria gained the additional title of Empress of India in 1876. The royal title changed to its current form in 1921 when 26 counties of the island of Ireland became a separate state. With the dissolution of the Empire, the Queen became head of a multi-continental, multiracial Commonwealth that ceased to be described as British in 1949. The elasticity of the borders of the United Kingdom was shown in 1955 when an all-party commission recommended incorporating Malta into the United Kingdom rather than granting it independence. The Queen's full title today is: Elizabeth the Second, by the Grace of God, of the United Kingdom of Great Britain and Northern Ireland and of Her other Realms and Territories Queen, Head of the Commonwealth, Defender of the Faith.

There is no need for a democracy to have a single identity or uniform institutions; Switzerland is an outstanding example of a multinational confederation. A healthy democracy needs multiple political identities to be complementary rather than conflicting, and parties competing for votes throughout the United Kingdom rather than appealing to a single nation. It also needs a consensus about the boundaries of the state. It is a symptom of bad health if nationalist parties win support with a programme demanding independence from the United Kingdom; this is compounded if there is no agreement about how such a dispute can be peacefully resolved.

6.1   Multiple Identities

A common description of the political institutions of the United Kingdom is that they are British. Another is that they are English, as in Walter Bagehot's classic book *The English Constitution*. The confusion of English and British identities reflects the fact that more than five-sixths of the United Kingdom's population lives in England. The terms England and Britain can be used in at least six different ways.

- England to refer to England (World Cup football competition).
- England to refer to Britain. England expects every that every man will do his duty (Admiral Nelson's Battle of Trafalgar message to seamen of 22 nationalities).
- England to refer to the United Kingdom (The Bank of England).
- England and Britain used interchangeably *(Alas, Alas for England: What Went Wrong for Britain,* a book by Louis Heren).
- Britain to refer to the United Kingdom (British Broadcasting Corporation).
- Britain to refer to more than the United Kingdom (British nationality).

When British people are asked to choose a single national identity from a list of alternatives, the replies differ substantially between the four parts of the United Kingdom. For the first time, the 2011 census included a question asking people to say whether they identified as English, Welsh, Scottish, Northern Irish, Irish or British. There was no consistency in the choice of identity among people living in any of the four nations of the United Kingdom. In England 58 per cent identified themselves as English, in Wales 58 per cent said they were Welsh and in Scotland 62 per cent saw themselves as Scots. In England and Wales one-sixth of respondents gave their primary identity as British and in Scotland one in twelve did so. Because of its history, there is no majority for any identity in Northern Ireland. Among Protestants, 81 per cent said they were British while among Catholics only 13 per cent did so. Reciprocally, among Catholics 82 per cent identified themselves as Irish or Northern Irish.

The logic of a multinational kingdom is that people can have both a national and a British identity, and an individual's sense of identity can vary with context. For example, a person can identify as British when abroad, by their nation in World Cup football and with their city when in their home nation. The British Election Survey asks whether people have a national or British identity or hold both identities. A plurality reply that they feel equally British and English, Scots or Welsh. Tolerance of multiple identities avoids the friction that would arise from any attempt to homogenize a heterogeneous population to a single national identity.

Immigration from Commonwealth countries on four continents has given official recognition to a variety of ways of differentiating Black and Minority Ethnic (BAME) Britons from each other. In the 2011 census, questions distinguished between 18 ethnic nationality groups; five racial groups; and dozens of religions. In England and Wales, 80.5 per cent of respondents described themselves as white British, and an additional 5.5 per cent as White with a non-UK nationality. The second-largest category was the 7.5 per cent ethnic Asians; this included people who said they were ethnically Indian, Pakistani, Bangladeshi, Chinese or other Asian. People coming from Africa, the Caribbean and other continents were 3.3 per cent of respondents; Arabs and others 1.0 per cent; and individuals who described themselves as of mixed race 2.2 per cent. Many official forms appear in multiple Asian languages as well as English, Welsh and Gaelic.

The European Union sought to promote identification with Europe by automatically conferring European citizenship on all citizens of member states including the United Kingdom in the 1992 Maastricht Treaty. However, Britain's leaders did not try to promote this policy, whereas German leaders have seen a European identity as replacing their country's nationalist past. The extent to which Britons have a feeling of being European varies with the way in which a question is asked. When the Eurobarometer asked Britons whether they saw themselves as Europeans, the one-third who said they did was well below the big majority of respondents in continental European countries. When the 2017 British Election Survey asked people to select their primary identity from a list that included European as an option, only four of the 2194 respondents identified as European.

A multiplicity of national identities is not a symptom of political ill health. Americans have multiple political identities derived from geography, such as being a Texan and an American; ethnicity, Irish-American; or race, Afro-American. Up to a point, the confusion between British and English identity can mask the fact that the dominance of England in the population of the United Kingdom places power in the hands of politicians and parties that represent voters in England.

6.2   A Unitary Crown Without Uniformity

The United Kingdom is a unitary state because Acts of the UK Parliament determine which policies and resources are retained in Westminster and which are delegated to devolved institutions in Scotland, Wales and Northern Ireland. The powers of each are determined unilaterally by the UK government, and each set is different. The concurrent jurisdiction of devolved institutions and UK authorities does not make them equal. The powers of the Scottish Parliament, the Welsh Senedd and the Northern Ireland Executive are far less than states in the American federal system, each of which has substantial taxing, legislative and judicial powers. Westminster retains the power to suspend, re-organize or revoke the powers of devolved institutions, and it has exercised all three in Northern Ireland.

Political institutions vary in their geographical coverage. Only a few Whitehall departments act solely on behalf of the United Kingdom as a whole: the Foreign, Commonwealth and Development Office, the Ministry of Defence, and the Department of International Trade. The taxing and spending policies of the Treasury have an impact on the economy of all parts of the United Kingdom, and it allocates the principal amount of revenue of local authorities and devolved national parliaments. Since pensions and unemployment benefits are uniform throughout the United Kingdom, the Department of Work and Pensions serves people throughout the United Kingdom.

The great majority of Whitehall departments have a mixture of responsibilities, some covering the whole of the United Kingdom, others Great Britain, England and Wales, while some concentrate on England (Gallagher 2018). For example, the Home Office is responsible for immigration and security for the whole of the United Kingdom, for policing in England and Wales, and for the Fire Service in England. The measures for dealing with coronavirus announced in Downing Street by the prime minister and the secretary of state for Health and Social Care apply only to

England. Health policies are separately decided by devolved governments in Scotland, Wales and Northern Ireland. Cabinet reshuffles regularly readjust the territorial scope of departments.

There are separate Cabinet ministers for Scotland, Wales and Northern Ireland. Each minister is officially described as representing territorial interests within the UK government and advocating UK government policies at the national level. Their political status is low; in the official ranking of 20 Cabinet ministers they are placed sixteenth, seventeenth and eighteenth.

Devolution. While Scotland, Wales and Northern Ireland had long had nationalist movements, these did not begin to gain traction in British politics until 1974. Labour had counted on winning a big majority of MPs in Scotland and Wales in order to win control of British government, but in two elections that year the Scottish National Party (SNP) and Plaid Cymru in Wales gained 14 MPs and Labour governed without a working majority. The Labour government responded by promoting Acts of Parliament that devolved limited policy responsibilities to elected assemblies in Scotland and Wales. In national referendums in 1979, the Westminster proposals were rejected by a big majority in Wales and by an insufficient turnout of voters in Scotland.

A period of 18 years in opposition to a Conservative government made the Labour party more strongly committed to devolution. It assumed that devolved institutions would neutralize support for nationalist parties in Scotland and Wales and assist Labour in winning UK general elections. When Labour won the 1997 election it promptly called referendums on the principle of introducing devolved institutions of government. In Scotland 74.3 per cent voted in favour and in Wales 50.3 per cent. Acts of Parliament promptly authorized the election of Scottish and Welsh parliaments, and devolved governments were established in Edinburgh and Cardiff in 1999. In Northern Ireland the 1998 Good Friday Agreement established a devolved power-sharing government. Instead of control of government rotating between major parties, a government can only be formed by ministries being distributed to parties in proportion to their share of the vote.

The term devolution emphasizes the determination of Westminster politicians to maintain the United Kingdom as a unitary state rather than allowing it to become a federal state. Acts of the UK Parliament decide the powers that devolved parliaments have and devolved bodies have no authority to amend these Acts. Whitehall welcomed getting rid of administering health, education and local government policies on terms differing from England and shedding nation-specific policies such as Scottish tourism and the use of the Welsh language (Bulpitt 1986). Devolution was intended to consign nationalist parties to the Celtic fringes by satisfying demands that did not interfere with areas of policy that the UK government considered important, such as managing the economy. In short, the aim was to devolve and forget.

Today, there is an asymmetry in the relationship between devolved governments and the UK government. Politicians in devolved governments see themselves as partners with Westminster in a quasi-federal political system in which they are partners with Westminster in the government of the United Kingdom. However, this perspective does not take into account the United Kingdom's most populous nation, England. England does not have a devolved Parliament and English public opinion favours keeping the government of England in the hands of the United Kingdom government (Russell and Sheldon 2018: 106). Of the 650 MPs in the United Kingdom Parliament, 533 sit for English constituencies. This is not a sign of democratic ill health but the opposite: it is the consequence of holding democratic elections in a multinational state in which England has more than five-sixths of the population.

6.3   From a British Party System to Four National Systems

In a healthy democratic political system, party competition contributes to the unity of the political system because parties compete and win votes by advocating policies that are of common concern throughout the whole of Britain. A general election can change control of the government, but the boundaries of the country remain secure. In competing for control of the British government, the Conservative and Labour parties have always been unselfconsciously British parties contesting seats throughout Great Britain.

The first-past-the-post system gives nationalist parties the opportunity to return some MPs from the national constituencies they do contest. For a relatively brief period between 1885 and 1918, every general election posed a threat to the unity of the United Kingdom because Ireland returned 101 MPs and Irish nationalists sometimes held the balance of power at Westminster. After the Irish Free State was established in 1921, Northern Ireland had only 12 seats, and until the 1970s its Unionist MPs invariably voted with the Conservatives. At the 2019 election six different nationalist parties divided 70 Westminster seats in Scotland, Northern Ireland and Wales.

Class divisions a force for cross-national integration. Because class divisions exist in all four nations of the United Kingdom, parties can compete for control of the UK government by emphasizing economic and social issues common to all parts of the United Kingdom. When Labour governments took industries into public ownership, they were nationalized on behalf of the UK government. The Conservative party's 'one nation' appeal was addressed to voters in all parties of the United Kingdom. In the past politicians with Scottish links have been well represented in Westminster. Winston Churchill represented Dundee for 14 years until defeated by a Prohibition Party candidate.

The conventional view of party politics in the 1960s was summed up by Peter Pulzer (1967: 98), 'Class is the basis of British party politics; all else is embellishment and detail'. Although widely quoted, the statement fell short of being completely accurate when it was made. The Conservatives have always needed a significant fraction of working-class votes to win control of government, and under Harold Wilson the Labour party began to increase its middle-class support. At the 1964 election, all 630 seats in the House of Commons were held by one of the three British parties. Whether MPs voiced their views in an English, Welsh, Scots or Ulster accent, all voted in accord with a British party's whip.

The decline in class and party identification has had different consequences in the four nations of the United Kingdom. In England the chief beneficiary has been the Liberal Democrats, a party that campaigns and wins seats throughout Britain. Because England and Britain are virtually interchangeable in Westminster, there is no need for an English nationalist party. At the 2019 election, the English Democratic Party, which campaigns for an English Parliament, finished twenty-eighth, winning only 0.005 per cent of the vote in England. The United Kingdom Independence Party opposed the European Union as British nationalists, waving the Union Jack in defence of British sovereignty. In the 2019 European Parliament election its successor, the Brexit Party, won 30 per cent of Scottish and Welsh seats as well as being the leading party in England.

Devolved politics are democratic but different. There are six ways in which the elections of parliaments in Scotland, Wales and Northern Ireland differ from the election of the UK Parliament. Most obviously, the government of the United Kingdom is not at stake. Secondly, the dates of elections are separate from the election of the Westminster Parliament. Thirdly, proportional representation is used to award seats to parties. Fourthly, the electorates are radically different, since the right to cast a ballot is determined by residence; thus, more than 90 per cent of the UK electorate is ineligible to vote in an election in a devolved nation. Fifthly, the Scottish, Welsh and Northern Ireland media that produce political news place a premium on reporting the activities of the devolved parliaments and governments. Finally, the results are different; nationalist parties are major parties and often participate or control devolved governments.

In the initial election of the Scottish Parliament in 1999, the SNP gained 27 per cent of the votes and seats compared with gaining 8 per cent of Scotland's seats with 22 per cent of the vote in the preceding Westminster election. The first two devolved elections resulted in Labour–Liberal Democratic coalition governments. After the vote of both coalition partners dropped in 2007 and the Scottish National Party won a plurality of seats, it formed a minority government and has governed on its own since. After the SNP won an absolute majority in the Scottish Parliament in 2011, it secured the consent of the UK government to hold an independence referendum. In the 2014 ballot, 55 per cent voted for remaining in the United Kingdom and 45 per cent for Scottish independence.

Plaid Cymru won just under 10 per cent of the Welsh vote in the 1997 Westminster election but two years later won 30 per cent of the vote in the first devolved election. Labour has come first in seats in all five devolved Welsh elections but has never won an absolute majority. It has alternated between leading a single-party minority government, a coalition with the Liberal Democrats, or on one occasion a coalition with Plaid Cymru. While usually finishing second, Plaid Cymru has never won as much as one-third of the 60 seats. It has been successful in using its vote to get the Welsh government to adopt measures promoting the Welsh language and culture. In 2020 the Welsh National Assembly changed its name to the Welsh equivalent: Senedd Cymru.

In Northern Ireland no party wins a majority, and six parties plus three independents have won seats. In the six elections since 1998, the two hardline parties, the Democratic Unionist Party (DUP) and Sinn Fein, are almost equal in seats and the same is true of the second-largest Unionist and Irish nationalist parties. The Alliance Party, the chief party attracting votes across the Protestant/Catholic divide, finishes fifth. Whereas Sinn Fein refuses to occupy the seats it wins in UK elections on the grounds that Northern Ireland should be governed by Dublin, it does participate in the Northern Ireland government, which it sees as a step towards the unification of Ireland. Under the terms of the Good Friday Agreement, the leading Unionist party and the leading Republican party must agree to participate in a power-sharing executive for a government to be formed. In 2020 there was a four-party coalition government.

The United Kingdom's four different national party systems operate at two different levels (Table 6.1). For British parties, competition for seats in the Westminster Parliament is by far the more important because it determines which party governs the United Kingdom and because nationalist parties do not nominate seats in England. Control of UK government alternates between the two major British parties, the Conservatives and Labour. Generations of entrenchment in Wales give British parties nine-tenths of the Welsh vote. By contrast, in Scotland the SNP has become the dominant party, winning a majority of Westminster seats at the last three general elections. The Labour party, previously returning a majority

Table 6.1   The United Kingdom's four national party systems

| | *Westminster Parliament, 2019* | | | |
	England *%*	*Wales* *%*	*Scotland* *%*	*N.Ireland* *%*
Conservative	47.2	36.1	25.1	0.7
Labour	33.9	40.9	18.6	0.0
Liberal Democrat	12.4	6.0	9.5	0.0
(British parties)	*(100.0)*	*(90.1)*	*(55.0)*	*(0.7)*
Nationalist	n.a.	9.9	45.0	99.3
	Devolved parliaments			
	N.a.	*2016*	*2016*	*2017*
Conservative		21.2	22.0	0.3
Labour		34.7	22.6	0
Liberal Democrat		7.7	7.8	0
(British parties)		*(79.5)*	*(53.5)*	*(0.3)*
Nationalist/Republican		20.5	46.5	44.7
NI Unionists				55.0
(National parties)		*(20.5)*	*(46.5)*	*(99.7)*

Source House of Commons Library Briefing Paper CBP 7529 2nd ed. In Scotland and Wales devolved vote is for constituency candidates of Scottish MPs since 1959, took only one seat there in 2019. Since the Conservative government abolished the old Northern Ireland Parliament at Stormont in 1972, no British party has elected any of the Northern Ireland MPs at Westminster.

The Brexit referendum produced conflicting results within the United Kingdom too. Whereas in 1975 all four nations approved the United Kingdom's membership in the European Union, in 2016 there were majorities in England and Wales to leave the EU while in Scotland and Northern Ireland to remain. London was an outlier in England: its vote to remain in the EU was almost as high as that in Scotland. The two million majority in England for leaving the EU determined the United Kingdom outcome. Just as the EU negotiated the United Kingdom's membership exclusively with the Westminster government, so it accepted Westminster's notification of withdrawal on behalf of all parts of the United Kingdom.

For nationalist parties, competition for seats in their national parliaments is more important than for Westminster seats, because it provides opportunities for influencing devolved public services and a platform to promote their case for self-government. In Scotland the SNP has been in control of the government since 2007, thereby become the chief governing party. The power-sharing requirement for forming a Northern Ireland government has meant that the DUP and Sinn Fein are assured of a permanent place in government; they campaign to consolidate support in their respective communities for the conflicting causes of union with Great Britain and the unification of Ireland. British parties have maintained control of the Welsh Executive since Plaid Cymru's signature policy—promoting the Welsh language in an electorate which is three-quarters monoglot English-speakers—is a liability in winning votes.

All parties have an incentive to demand more powers and money for their devolved government and to criticize the Westminster government for decisions it takes. Nationalist parties have a clear solution for getting rid of friction with Westminster: it is to become independent. Unionist parties are handicapped, because they must defend the sovereignty of the UK government while simultaneously criticizing it for specific actions. Moreover, they must be cautious about offering special advantages to devolved nations so as not to offend their base in England. In the 2019 general election, 91 per cent of the Conservative vote came from England, 90 per cent of the Liberal Democrat vote and 89 per cent of Labour's vote.

The Conservative Party has the advantage in appealing for the votes of those against independence because they have traditionally been strongly Unionist and critical of devolution. However, the unpopularity of English prime ministers such as Margaret Thatcher and Boris Johnson is a handicap. The Conservatives poll 10–20 percentage points lower in Wales and Scotland than in England, and like other British parties do not compete in Northern Ireland. Since going into opposition at Westminster in 2010, the Labour Party has lost more than half its vote in Scotland and lots of seats to the centre-left SNP. In Wales Labour has benefited by the collapse of support for the Liberal Democrats.

It is a positive sign of democratic health when parties in favour of the United Kingdom win big majorities in both Westminster and devolved elections. This is only the case in Wales, where British parties win four-fifths of the vote in the election of the Welsh Senedd and nine-tenths of the vote for the UK Parliament. In Scotland three Unionist parties divide a majority of the vote, while different parties the SNP comes first in votes and seats in both Westminster and Scottish Parliament elections. Northern Ireland is distinctive because its Democratic Unionist Party, founded by Dr. Ian Paisley, is staunchly Unionist but also a Northern Ireland nationalist party; it tactically supported and then opposed a Conservative minority government in the 2017–2019 UK Parliament depending on how the government's policies affected Northern Ireland.

6.4   The Contingency of Consent

A healthy democracy, first of all, requires consent to democratic institutions. The UK government meets this condition. Nationalist parties have shown their consent by participating in Westminster elections even though they do not want to participate in the British government. Moreover, each can claim that devolved parliaments are more democratic than the UK Parliament because their lower ratio of voters to elected representatives makes them closer to the people and the use of proportional representation to elect devolved representatives is fairer than Westminster's first-past-the-post electoral system. The SNP has proposed that an independent Scotland would increase the variety of democratic institutions in use, for example, holding citizen assemblies to discuss major issues of policy.

Northern Ireland is a qualified democracy; the political institutions established to seek an end to civil war differ fundamentally from the Westminster model. Voters elect members of the Northern Ireland Assembly by a single-transferable-vote similar to that in the Republic of Ireland. Control of government cannot rotate between major parties. Instead, there is mandatory power-sharing. This differs from Dutch-style consociational government in which parties are free to bargain about forming coalitions and control of government can change between major parties. The Democratic Unionist Party has always won the First Ministership in every election and since the second election Sinn Fein, an Irish Republican party, has taken the post of Deputy First Minister. Disagreements within the Executive about such issues as policing and Irish language use have four times led to the devolved government being suspended and Westminster government temporarily assuming full control of Northern Ireland government.

A second critical condition of a healthy democracy is that all parties consent to the same definition of its boundaries. Consent is taken for granted in a nation-state. Because the United Kingdom is a multinational state, more is required: there must be a concurring consensus in all four nations of the United Kingdom. Up to a point both Scottish and Welsh nationalists accept the geographical boundaries of their devolved governments as defining the territory for which independence is sought. The nation is defined as the people who live within these boundaries, an inclusive definition that does not discriminate on grounds of race, language or religion. The population of Wales is 73 per cent Welsh-born and 27 per cent born in England or elsewhere and in Scotland it is 83 per cent Scottish-born.

The relationship between devolved Welsh institutions and the UK government has been relatively healthy, because Plaid Cymru, the Welsh nationalist party, has averaged barely one-fifth of the regional vote in five elections for the Welsh Senedd. Although it supports the principle of a referendum giving Welsh residents the opportunity to vote for independence, it does not push for a vote that would almost certainly reject the idea. Plaid Cymru promotes Welsh language use, but as only 18 per cent of voters say that they can speak Welsh, it has the gradualist objective of Wales becoming a bilingual nation through education.

There is an unhealthy condition in Northern Ireland because its major parties disagree about whether it should be part of the United Kingdom or the Republic of Ireland. The current border of Northern Ireland with the Republic was drawn in 1921 as a peace line separating Irish nation-alists and Ulster Unionists while the Withdrawal Agreement between the European Union and the UK government has created an open border between Northern Ireland and the Republic and a customs border between Great Britain and Northern Ireland. The Irish Republican move-ment has never recognized the border and has a two-pronged strategy for achieving the unification of the whole of the island of Ireland with a ballot in one hand and an ArmaLite weapon in the other.

The British government has sought to encourage Irish Republicans to work through lawful institutions by offering to hold a referendum on Irish unification. The 1998 Northern Ireland Act states that a referendum on the border would be called 'If at any time it appears likely to him [that is, the UK minister for Northern Ireland] that a majority of those voting would express a wish that Northern Ireland should cease to be part of the United Kingdom and form part of a united Ireland'. There is no statutory provision for allowing Ulster Unionists a referendum to reaffirm Northern Ireland's membership in the United Kingdom. Ulster Unionists have been ready to defend the border by taking up arms under British command or in locally organized paramilitary forces.

There is no agreement between the UK government and the SNP-controlled Scottish government about when a second referendum on Scottish independence can be called. The 1998 Scotland Act specifically declares that the Scottish Parliament is not allowed to legislate on matters reserved to Westminster such as 'the Union of the Kingdoms of Scot-land and England'. This power is exclusively in the hands of Westminster. The UK government agreed to the SNP government's demand for an independence referendum in 2014 as a once-in-a-generation vote. The majority voted to remain in the United Kingdom.

Because securing Scottish independence is the primary purpose of the SNP, it includes a commitment in its election manifestos to hold another referendum on independence. The justification is that a new political situ-ation has arisen: The United Kingdom's withdrawal from the European Union has taken Scotland out of the EU even though a clear majority in Scotland voted to remain. The demand for another vote is also consistent with opinion polls that early in 2021 indicated that a majority of Scots would now vote for independence. The UK Conservative government has refused to approve a second independence referendum, and the British Labour party endorses this view too. The SNP First Minister of Scot-land, Nicola Sturgeon, is under pressure from within her party to hold a 'legal referendum' in order to avoid the problems that Catalunya faced when it held a referendum on independence from Spain that was illegal under the Spanish Constitution. For the UK government and courts to declare a referendum Act of the Scottish Parliament illegal would raise the temperature in a feverish political situation.

Westminster sees the government of the United Kingdom as a unitary state in which the right to make decisions is concentrated in Whitehall and Parliament. It claims it is acting in the national interest as defined by issues that ministers see primarily in the context of London, the national capital, and their own constituencies. It did not intend devolution to create a dialogue between Westminster and governments in Edinburgh, Cardiff and Belfast to discuss their views on UK policies. The object was to insulate Westminster from the activities of devolved governments in three parts of the United Kingdom. The fact that this hasn't happened has led Boris Johnson to describe devolution as a 'disaster' in remarks to Conservative MPs in November 2019. Ex-Prime Minister Gordon Brown, a Scot and a Labour Unionist, has described what is now happening as 'threatening the end of the United Kingdom' (2021).

Studies of the breakdown in the health of democratic states emphasize that a critical point is reached when politicians responsible for defending existing institutions no longer believe they can do so successfully (Mounk 2018). The confidence of Westminster politicians in the maintenance of the United Kingdom is given by an Ipsos-MORI survey (Fig. 6.1). It asked how likely MPs thought it was that in the next ten years Scotland, Wales and/or Northern Ireland would leave the United Kingdom. The respondents, who predominantly represented English constituencies, differ in their expectations by party as well as nation.

There is agreement among both Conservative and Labour MPs that it is very unlikely that Wales would ever produce a referendum majority to leave the United Kingdom. There is uncertainty among both groups about the future of Northern Ireland. More than half of Labour MPs see Irish unification as likely in the next decade, while only one-quarter of Conservative MPs do so. The biggest disagreement is about Scotland. Among Labour MPs, who have seen their once-triumphant Scottish party reduced to a single MP at Westminster, two-thirds think Scottish independence likely. Among Conservative MPs, hopeful that their party will prosper electorally in Scotland as the defender of the Union, only one in ten think Scotland is likely to become independent by 2030.

Q. In your opinion, over the next ten years how unlikely is each of the following?

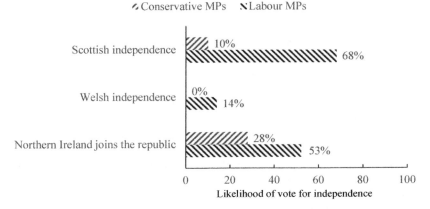

Fig. 6.1 MPs' expectations of the United Kingdom breaking up (*Source* Ipsos MORI survey of MPs, January–February 2020, as reported in Wager 2020)

Movements seeking to challenge the status quo must be patient in pursuit of their goals, and some never reach them (Rose 1997). Plaid Cymru was founded in 1925 and needed 41 years before winning its first seat in the Westminster Parliament. The Scottish National Party was founded in 1934 and won control of a devolved government 73 years later. The movement for an independent and united Ireland has its roots in the nineteenth century. Its motto is: *Tiocfaidh ár lá* (Our day will come).

REFERENCES

Aughey, Arthur. 2018. England and Britain in Historical Perspective. In *Governing England*, ed. M. Kenny, I. McLean, and A. Paun, 27–44. Oxford: Oxford University Press.

Brown, Gordon. 2021. The PM's Choice Is Between a Modern Reformed UK and a Failed State. *Daily Telegraph*, January 25.

Bulpitt, Jim. 1986. *Territory and Power in the United Kingdom*. Manchester: Manchester University Press.

Gallagher, Jim. 2018. The Ghost in the Machine? The Government of England. In *Governing England*, ed. M. Kenny, I. McLean, and A. Paun, 69–90. Oxford: Oxford University Press.

Mounk, Yascha. 2018. *The People vs. Democracy: Why Our Freedom Is in Danger and How to Save It*. Cambridge, MA: Harvard University Press.

Pulzer, Peter. 1967. *Political Representation and Elections in England*. London: George Allen and Unwin.

Rose, Richard. 1971. *Governing Without Consensus: An Irish Perspective*. London: Faber and Faber.

Rose, Richard. 1997. How Patient Are People in Post-Communist Societies? *World Affairs* 159 (3): 130–144.

Russell, Meg, and Jack Sheldon. 2018. An English Parliament: An Idea Whose Time Has Come? In *Governing England*, ed. M. Kenny, I. McLean, and A. Paun, 91–114. Oxford: Oxford University Press.

Wager, Alan. 2020. The Union: Do MPs Expect a Break Up? July 17. https://ukandeu.ac.uk/the-union-do-mps-expect-a-break-up/.

CHAPTER 7

An Unbalanced Constitution

Democratic governance requires the rule of law to prevent a popularly elected government from using its power to subvert free elections, deliver public services unfairly or corruptly, or avoid accountability for its actions. The rules setting limits on what an elected government can and can't do are normally stated in a Basic Law (*Grundgesetz*), the term that Germany uses to describes its constitution. Basic laws are superior to an ordinary Act of Parliament and a constitution empowers courts to decide disputes about whether the government of the day has exceeded its constitutional powers. Whereas the electorate holds the government accountable for its overall performance, courts hold the government to account for a single action.

In a democratic constitution there is normally a tripartite institutional division between the executive branch in control of government; a parliament that represents voters; and courts that ensure the executive and parliament act within their constitutional powers. The interaction of these three institutions creates a system of checks and balances. In a presidential system, the representative assembly is separately elected. In parliamentary democracies with coalition governments, the government depends on the maintenance of a coalition of parliamentary parties. If the government of the day seeks to amend the constitution or pack the constitutional court

© The Author(s), under exclusive license to Springer Nature Switzerland AG 2021
R. Rose, *How Sick Is British Democracy?*
Challenges to Democracy in the 21st Century,
https://doi.org/10.1007/978-3-030-73123-6_7

to reduce checks on its power, as in contemporary Hungary and Poland, this is a symptom of a threat to the life of democracy.

The British Constitution is different because it developed in an undemocratic era and has evolved rather than being replaced by a modern democratic constitution as in Germany in 1949, France in 1958 and Sweden in 1975. In the aftermath of the seventeenth-century English civil war, Parliament imposed checks on the absolute power of the monarchy and established a separation of powers between the monarchy, the House of Lords and the House of Commons, a mixed system of government in which each could check the other and none was democratically accountable. Parliament became the highest court of the land before democracy took hold. A. V. Dicey (1885) defined the central tenet of the Constitution as parliamentary sovereignty: as long as the House of Commons and the House of Lords agreed, Parliament could make or repeal any Act free of any constraint of the courts or the monarchy. The 1911 House of Lords Act removed the Lords as a check on the Commons.

In Britain democratization did not require the cumbersome procedure of writing a new constitution or meeting onerous requirements to amend an existing one. Instead, it was achieved by a succession of Acts of Parliament that gradually led to universal suffrage and elections deciding which party controlled government. The creation of party government made MPs in the majority dependent for re-election on supporting the government in major constitutional disputes. Instead of Parliament being a check on the executive, the government of the day gained the unconstrained power of parliamentary sovereignty. Whereas courts in most democracies can claim constitutional legitimacy, the British government can claim that it has political power to decide constitutional issues by a single vote in the House of Commons because of its electoral legitimacy.

Instead of a written constitution, the United Kingdom has an unwritten constitution; there is no single document that summarizes the accumulation over many centuries of rules, customs and conventions that are referred to collectively as the country's constitution. In the words of an Edwardian journalist, 'We live under a system of tacit understandings. But the understandings themselves are not always understood' (Low 1914: 12).

An unwritten constitution makes it difficult for judges to rule on constitutional cases. If a case involves whether the government has acted within the terms laid down in an Act of Parliament, judges can relate what has been done to a written statute. By contrast, if the issue is whether the government of the day has acted within the rules of an unwritten consti-tution, there can be a variety of norms, customs and conventions that each side can invoke. If judges decide against the government of the day, they can be accused by politicians and the media of interfering in politics by refusing to respect the legitimacy of an elected government.

The British Constitution is unbalanced by the lack of clear constitu-tional constraints, and the courts are not so much separate from the government of the day as they are distant. Given the presumption that the government of the day has the right to exercise parliamentary sovereignty, the relationship between the government and the courts is healthiest when no political dispute arises about the constitutionality of govern-ment action. Disputes are infrequent because ministers, and even more their civil servants, have internalized norms about what government can and cannot do.

In a healthy democracy, competing parties can dispute particular public policies, but there is a consensus about basic constitutional laws and the role of an independent judiciary in enforcing constitutional rules and resolving disputes by orderly means. It is a sign of political ill health when constitutional disputes arise and the government of the day claims it has the right to act because it commands the support of an elected majority in Parliament. In the words of the eighteenth-century radical Tom Paine, 'Where the distinction between the constitution and the government is not observed, there is in effect no constitution.' Thus, when complaints arise about the government's powers without a judicial resolution complainants may turn to peaceful or not so peaceful means to resolve a conflict.

7.1   Politicians Are the Judges of What They Can Do

The preamble of a constitution normally identifies the source of its polit-ical authority. The most emulated democratic example is the American Constitution of 1787; it starts with the words 'We, the people'. The preambles of constitutions from France to Japan repeat this democratic language. Federal constitutions can include a reference to geographical regions and/or ethnic groups. The preamble of the Irish Constitution starts, 'In the Name of the Most Holy Trinity, from Whom is all authority and to Whom, as our final end, all actions both of men and States must be referred, We, the people of Eire …'. By contrast, UK Acts of Parliament state that they are an expression of the Crown in Parliament, a phrase that combines the pre-democratic authority of the reigning monarch with that of a democratically elected House of Commons.

In *The Law of the Constitution*, A. V. Dicey rejected the American idea of a constitution based on checks and balances between the executive, the legislature and the courts. Dicey based what he called the English Constitution on the doctrine that Parliament had the right to make or unmake any law and neither the monarch nor the courts could override what it did. Dicey's doctrine treated ministers as agents of Parliament, but in the decades that followed party government reversed the relationship. Party discipline results in MPs voting as agents of the whips of the governing party. Many Acts of Parliament delegate to ministers the power to make secondary laws to implement and enforce policies. Of approximately 3500 Statutory Instruments issued by the government each year, fewer than one-third are subject to parliamentary scrutiny, and only a very small percentage are rejected or amended. A former Conservative Lord Chancellor, Lord Hailsham, argued in a 1976 BBC lecture that there is no barrier to the British government becoming an elective dictatorship.

Instead of looking to the courts and constitutional amendments to advance its goals, the British Labour movement has always favoured the Dicey's doctrine of the unchecked power of the government of the day. Its leaders have wanted a Labour government to be free to enact socialist laws that the courts could not invalidate. It has seen judges as representing a public-school-educated and capitalist class likely to make decisions unfavourable to trade unions. Social and employment laws of Labour governments have often created tribunals separate from the courts to hear disputes about individual claims of their statutory rights.

Downing Street can cover itself against challenges in the courts by 'leaning on' its chief law officer to give the opinion it wants. Tony Blair wanted an international legal opinion to justify sending British troops to join the American-led invasion of Iraq in 2003 and claimed there was good evidence that Iraq was making weapons of mass destruction. Blair's attorney general, Lord Goldsmith, twice advised that, in the absence of strong factual evidence, an invasion would not meet the conditions for invading Iraq specified in a UN Resolution. After being told to consult with American security officials about the legal evidence, Goldsmith concluded that evidence made the invasion lawful. An official inquiry established by Blair's successor, Gordon Brown, concluded that the government had stretched evidence 'to the outer limits' and that the war was unnecessary (Chilcot 2016).

Because the British Constitution developed when the government was not democratic, it lacks a constitutional guarantee of individual rights like the American Constitution's Bill of Rights and the statement on inalienable human rights in Germany's Basic Law. Individual rights were first given the authority of an international treaty in 1951 by the UK government signing the European Convention on Human Rights. In the 1960s British citizens became formally eligible to claim these rights from the UK government by presenting a case to the European Court of Human Rights in Strasbourg. In response to racial discrimination against immigrants from the New Commonwealth, a Labour government adopted the Human Rights Act in 1998. It incorporated into British law individual rights enumerated in the European Convention. While the courts can declare a British Act of Parliament incompatible with the European Convention, it cannot void the British Act on that basis. The government of the day retains the power to countermand the judicial interpretation of the rights of Britons by amending the Human Rights Act. The 2019 Conservative party election manifesto proposed to update the Human Rights Act.

Judges traditionally saw judicial review as a process of upholding the letter of the law rather than interpreting Acts of Parliament broadly in their political and social context. The Whitehall practice in drafting legislation is to give ministers the power to act in ways that they deem reasonable. The courts have hesitated to reject what a minister regards as reasonable even if it is unsupported by any evidence. Whereas legislation in countries with a written constitution may be required to justify actions by citing a relevant constitutional clause, this is not possible in Westminster. A former head of the civil service privately explained how the government of the day decides how to exercise its authority: 'We make it up as we go along' (Rose 2001: 15).

For more than a century politicians and the courts have found mutually convenient Dicey's dictum that the courts should not interfere in the actions of the government of the day. Judges have maintained their standing as a non-political body by deferring to Parliament as the institution deciding whether an action of the government is consistent with the norms of an unwritten constitution. The appointment of judges was not a matter of partisan dispute, and lawyers and judges became, in effect, a self-regulating profession; their arcane language and procedures have shielded their activities and privileges from scrutiny. The result has been described by a very senior civil servant as enabling 'the executive government in this country to enjoy a power and a freedom [from judicial restraint] which is unrivalled in the liberal democratic world' (Wass 1986: x).

In keeping with changes in society and the turnover of generations, judges have slowly begun to give up their insulation from the British political system by taking a wider view of their powers (Stevens 2003). In 1966 the highest court announced it would no longer be strictly bound by precedent and that in interpreting Acts of Parliament it would look beyond the text of the statute and take into account ministerial statements and parliamentary debates giving indications of the Act's intent. Judges have also begun making more demands on the government to produce evidence and give reasons for its decisions.

The power of the government of the day to avoid constraint was temporarily undermined when the Conservative government lost its parliamentary majority at the 2017 general election. In 2019 an unprecedented Act of Parliament imposed conditions on government action on a matter of major constitutional importance, withdrawal from the European Union. It required the prime minister to seek an extension of negotiations if no agreement on the terms of withdrawal could be reached by a previously set deadline. Boris Johnson sought to escape the effect of the Act by asking the Queen to prorogue Parliament so that it would be in recess for five weeks and return only when it was too late to challenge Johnson's Brexit policy.

In response to a request for judicial review of the prime minister's action, the UK Supreme Court showed it had teeth by invalidating prorogation. Invoking a decision that ruled against King James I in 1611, the UK Supreme Court ruled unanimously that Parliament was sovereign. If the prime minister could avoid scrutiny by Parliament for a lengthy period, this would undermine the accountability of the government to Parliament.

Prime Minister Johnson correctly described as political the Supreme Court's decision to nullify his action, since the court was intervening in a dispute between the government and Parliament. He could also have called it alien, since the Supreme Court was doing what courts in a foreign democracy would do, deciding whether the government was acting in keeping with a written constitution. Johnson grudgingly complied, sending Brussels an unsigned request to extend negotiations on Brexit by three months. Separately he sent a signed letter stating his objection to having to do so. A champion of Brexit, Jacob Rees-Mogg, described the judgement as a 'constitutional coup'.

Boris Johnson has tried to push the courts to revert to their traditional practice of judicial self-restraint. The Conservative election manifesto contained a pledge to establish a Constitution, Democracy and Rights Commission to recommend how to ensure that the courts do not use their power 'to conduct politics by another means'. The attorney general has criticized the courts for steadily encroaching on the rights of politicians and declared the need for the Crown in Parliament (that is, the governing party) to 'take back control' from judges (*Economist* 2020). In July 2020 Johnson approved the appointment of Lord Edward Faulks, a former Conservative minister of justice, to chair a panel to consider on what grounds courts should be able to review the exercise of constitutional powers by the government of the day. Vigorous attacks by Prime Minister Johnson and Home Secretary Patel on 'lefty lawyers' prompted 802 lawyers, including retired Supreme Court judges, to express deep concern about government attacks on 'lawyers seeking to hold the government to the law' (*Guardian* 2020).

Johnson extended the Dicey doctrine to international law when faced with the implications of the Withdrawal Agreement that he had signed with the European Commission to get Brexit done. It established a border for regulating customs checks on goods moving from Great Britain to Northern Ireland, because the latter continues to have an open border with the Republic of Ireland, an EU member state. In September 2020 the Conservative government introduced an Internal Market Bill authorizing it to repudiate this arrangement. The Northern Ireland minister, Brendan Lewis, admitted in Parliament, 'This does break international law in a very specific and limited way'.

The Johnson government's disregard for informal constitutional constraints led the government's chief law officer to resign. The former president of the Supreme Court, Lord Neuberger, described the government as on a slippery slope leading to dictatorship and tyranny. Former prime ministers John Major and Tony Blair jointly condemned the bill as killing trust in Britain. The government's attempt to apply Dicey's doctrine of sovereignty was not shot down in Westminster but in Brussels. The European Union made clear that it was unwilling to sign an agreement on future trade with the United Kingdom if the British government could cherry-pick which parts of a treaty it chose to follow and which to ignore.

Diagnosing the health of the United Kingdom's unwritten constitution by standards applicable to a country with a written constitution is hardly appropriate but it can be evaluated by democratic standards. Individual Britons now have rights that they can make the government of the day respect in specific cases. However, there are recurring symptoms of Conservative and Labour governments acting in ways that take advantage of the absence of constitutional laws that the courts can enforce. A perverse consequence of party government is that a majority of MPs in a democratically elected House of Commons are unwilling to check governmental abuses of its powers, while an undemocratically constituted House of Lords is. Party discipline delivered a Commons majority for the violation of international law by the Internal Market Bill, while the Lords delivered a big majority to remove the offending clause.

7.2   Constitutional Rules Are Not Politics as Usual

In the absence of a written constitution, there are no laws, rights or institutions that can be positively verified as constitutional or unconstitutional. The gap is filled by written commentaries on an unwritten constitution by law scholars and by judicial *obiter dicta*. As in countries with a written constitution, textbooks on the British Constitution have chapters about the composition and functions of Parliament, the Cabinet and government departments, public finance, and the relation of the citizen and the state. There are also chapters that are distinctly British concerning the Crown and the royal prerogative, the Commonwealth, and official secrets.

The customs and conventions that constitute the norms of the unwritten constitution are described as 'non-legal rules that are considered to be binding' (Marshall and Moodie 1959: 22), but are not enforceable by the courts. They include such conventions as an Act of Parliament requiring the signature of the Queen to become law and the Queen signing any measure approved by both Houses of Parliament. It is customary that, if a person is made a government minister and lacks a seat in Parliament, then he or she must win a Commons seat in a by-election or be appointed a member of the House of Lords in order to be personally accountable to Parliament. Conventions are easily altered. When Prime Minister Jim Callaghan was asked about the convention of collective Cabinet responsibility in 1977, he explained, 'I certainly think that the doctrine should apply, except in cases where I announce that it does not'.

Freedom from the constraints of a written constitution encourages Britain's governors to assume that what they do is legal, and discourages civil servants from raising legal doubts about actions that ministers want to take. Politicians' indifference to legal rules is reinforced by a big long-term shift in the occupational background of MPs. The proportion of MPs who started their political career by campaigning for votes has greatly increased, while the number who have been practising lawyers has almost halved in the past half-century. Among MPs elected in 2017, there were only 66 lawyers but 246 who had worked in political occupations (Cowley and Kavanagh 2018: Table 15). This creates a pool of MPs who are ready to criticize on political grounds judicial decisions they do not like. In the great majority of cases, such decisions enforce an Act of Parliament that ministers have the power to alter.

Amending Britain's unwritten constitution is much easier than altering a written one, which normally requires approval from multiple institutions and/or a super-majority in Parliament. By contrast, in Britain the procedure is the same as that for approving an Act of Parliament, such as the Cosmetic Surgery (Standards) Bill. A majority of one among MPs in parallel with the same majority in the House of Lords is sufficient to change basic laws or to endorse a new convention more suited to the government's convenience than an old convention. The governing party's whips can normally deliver that majority. The House of Lords can amend a bill but, if the government insists, it will not override a second Commons vote that removes the amendment and endorses what the government wants. A law professor has described the effect of the government's power to decide constitutional rules: 'The Constitution is what happens' (Griffith 1963).

In parliamentary debates about a government bill, MPs disagree on grounds of partisan values, fairness and practical effects. They do not question the government's legal right to put the bill forward. For example, when Conservatives talk about the injustice of inheritance tax and Labour adherents about the injustice of poverty, their remedy is not to go to the courts to seek justice. It is to gain a parliamentary majority to change laws. This pragmatic approach contrasts with that of the framers of the Indian Constitution, who pronounced that India was a social state. However, the social rights listed in Part IV of that constitution cannot be enforced by the courts or financed by the government of India.

The flexibility inherent in an unwritten constitution is often cited as a major advantage that compensates for the absence of formal constraints. In an emergency, the government can take unconventional actions that are illegal, that is, not authorized by an Act of Parliament. In dealing with the coronavirus epidemic, for example, the government can immediately alter or reverse regulations in response to changing data about the extent of infection and political pressures about the costs of its regulations. Its actions can be justified as in keeping with the need for 'a new practice, to meet a new emergency, a new condition of things'; this statement was made to the House of Commons in 1931 when a National Government coalition was formed in a time of financial crisis (quoted in Bradley et al. 2018: 27).

The courts hear cases in which there is a claim that a government department has acted *ultra vires*, a Latin phrase meaning acting beyond powers conferred by an Act of Parliament. When judges decide that the government is acting beyond its statutory powers, the court can stop it from doing so. The government can respond by adding a legislative clause that gives future authorization to a contested action or retrospective statutory authorization to a past violation. In an era of bulging statute books, the courts may also be asked to deal with conflicts between clauses in a new Act and old Acts dealing with the same subject.

A paperless constitution is not an obstacle to a healthy democracy as long as there is a consensus among parties and MPs about the customs and conventions controlling the British government. However, when disputes arise about a measure of constitutional significance, they require political resolution.

7.3   Constitutional Disputes Need Political Resolution

The great majority of the issues in British politics, such as the economy and social policy, rarely raise constitutional issues. However, from time to time a dispute arises about a constitutional matter such as the government using its powers in a novel way or failing to recognize individual rights. In the absence of an appeal to the courts, the aggrieved can proceed by trial and error, using a variety of strategies.

Demonstrations can give political visibility to a constitutional issue thanks to the media concentrating attention on what happens in London, whether what is described as a mass demonstration has a few thousand participants or tens of thousands. Strictly regulated demonstrations around Parliament Square are specially intended to capture the attention of MPs. Most demonstrations are not about constitutional issues but economic, social or foreign policy concerns. Demonstrators can seek the adoption of a policy, for example, a ban on nuclear weapons, or protest against a government measure such as coronavirus lockdowns. Whatever the size of a demonstration, a Parliament elected by tens of millions of voters can reject it.

The growth of the internet has led to the introduction of *e-petitions* to the House of Commons and the government. Procedures established in 2014 give any British citizen the right to file a petition electronically. It is reviewed by an official committee and as long as it calls for a specific action for which the UK government or the Commons is responsible it is published online. If the petition receives 10,000 valid signatures, the government must respond to its sponsors. If a petition gets 100,000 valid signatures, it will be considered for a debate in Parliament. By the beginning of 2021, 263 petitions have received a reply from the government and 46 have been debated in the Commons.

Lobbying MPs. Individual MPs can gain public attention for a constitutional issue, such as the protection of individual rights, but their actions cannot gain the resolution of an issue concerning constitutional rights; that is the prerogative of the government of the day. MPs who are shadow ministers of the Opposition party can be influential in adding a pledge to take action to the party's election manifesto. If the Opposition wins a general election, the new government can adopt a measure by invoking that it has a democratic right to do so. This lobbying tactic was effective in getting the inclusion of a commitment to hold a referendum on a major constitutional issue—the United Kingdom's membership of the European Union—in the 2015 Conservative party manifesto. When the Conservatives won an absolute majority, Eurosceptic MPs held Prime Minister David Cameron to deliver on the pledge, even though a BBC summary of the manifesto's key points found that commitment to a referendum came ninth and last in terms of the attention given issues during the election campaign.

Referendums as a higher court than Parliament. Whereas constitutional decisions by courts are made by non-elected judges, referendums make decisions by a democratic vote. A number of European constitutions specify that measures of constitutional significance such as joining the European Union must be put to the electorate in a referendum for confirmation. The use of the referendum was traditionally rejected as alien to the British doctrine of the sovereignty of Parliament. The first two referendums on constitutional issues were adopted for reasons of political expediency: the 1975 vote on the United Kingdom remaining a member of European institutions and the 2011 referendum endorsing the retention of the first-past-the-post electoral system.

British referendums have not been legally binding, but they can be politically binding. The need for Parliament to act did not arise in the case of the 1975 and 2011 referendums, because the majority vote confirmed the position of the government of the day. The 1979 referendum on an Act of Parliament authorizing Scottish devolution was unique in giving Scottish voters the binding authority to repeal the Act. It stated that, if 40 per cent of registered voters did not endorse it, then the government was obligated to repeal it. Even though a majority of Scots endorsed devolution, the Act was repealed because the majority voting for it fell more than 10 percentage points short of clearing the turnout barrier.

The Act of Parliament authorizing the European Union referendum did not contain a clause declaring the result would be binding nor did it set a turnout threshold. Nonetheless, the popular vote for leaving was accepted as politically binding by losers as well as winners. David Cameron as prime minister led the way, resigning within hours of the result being known. His successor, Theresa May, who had voted to remain in the EU, clinched her bid for Downing Street by pledging that she would carry out the referendum decision, saying 'Brexit means Brexit'. Even though a big majority of MPs had voted to remain in the EU, MPs accepted that referendum voters rather than Parliament should have the final say on this major constitutional issue. The bill giving the EU formal notice of withdrawal was approved by a vote of 493 to 110 MPs. Supporters of remaining in the EU gave their back-handed consent to popular sovereignty by campaigning for a second referendum that would offer voters the choice of withdrawing from the EU on terms negotiated with Brussels or reversing the 2016 referendum decision and remaining in the EU after all.

Chipping away at a political stone wall. The simplest response of the government to complaints about its abuse of constitutional powers is to stonewall, ignoring complaints or taking actions that evade accountability (see Sect. 5.3). Once the aggrieved become aware of this, they are left to chip away patiently at the stone wall with the help of investigative journalists, individual MPs and social media.

The Stephen Lawrence case is an example of what it takes to resolve a dispute involving a racist violation of human rights. In 1993 Lawrence, a Black 18-year-old, was wantonly assaulted and killed at a London bus stop by a group of White youths with racist opinions and police records. A friend of Lawrence who witnessed the attack identified two assailants, who were initially charged with murder; however, the case was dropped on the grounds that the witness's evidence was not reliable. The following year Stephen's parents brought a private prosecution, but the court ruled the witness's evidence inadmissible and the accused were found not guilty. A newly elected Labour Home secretary instituted a judicial inquiry, and in 1999 a report by Sir William Macpherson found police officers handling the Lawrence murder guilty of mistakes and actions that reflected the police force being imbued with institutional racism. After further lobbying by the Lawrence family and changes in the law, two assailants were retried in 2011. Nineteen years after the murder, the assailants were found guilty.

Trial and error. The British government has tried very different means, some democratic and others not, to resolve the fundamental constitutional dispute between Ulster Unionists and Irish Republicans about whether Northern Ireland should be part of the United Kingdom or the Republic of Ireland. The challenge started in 1921, when six predominantly Protestant counties of the Province of Ulster that had fought against Irish Republicans to remain within the United Kingdom secured their goal. An Act of Parliament established a devolved government modelled on *Westminster's democratic institutions.* MPs were elected by the first-past-the-post system to represent single-member constituencies. Executive power was in the hands of a Cabinet accountable to Parliament and unconstrained by the courts. Because the electorate divided along religious lines and Protestants were two-thirds of the province's electorate, there was no rotation of parties in government. Every election returned a Unionist government.

Peaceful demonstrations were launched in summer 1968 by Catholic groups seeking civil rights such as local government elections held on a democratic rather than a gerrymandered franchise. Unlike Southern civil rights demonstrators in the United States, the Northern Ireland group could not use the courts to complement their demonstrations because of the absence of statutory guarantees of civil rights (Rose 1976). The

Unionist government used its statutory powers to ban demonstrations and, when they went ahead, the police used force to break them up. That ended street demonstrations. It also gave the grievances of the civil rights demonstrators international publicity.

In response to political pressure from the British government to do something to quell disorder, the devolved Unionist government established a Review Body to examine local government, fixing its terms of reference to exclude civil rights complaints about electoral procedures falling short of British democratic standards (Macrory 1970: clause 7). Before the report could be completed, a peaceful but illegal protest in the Bogside district of Derry was followed by rioting in other parts of the province. Protestants, Catholics and Ulster police fired shots, and eight people were killed. The civil rights protest was succeeded by civil war.

The British government called a *referendum* on the Northern Ireland border in 1973 offering a choice between Northern Ireland remaining in the United Kingdom or joining the Republic of Ireland. Population differences between Protestants and Catholics made the result a foregone conclusion. That was the reason the British government called it: the result would give Ulster Unionists democratic evidence of support for the province remaining in the United Kingdom. For the same reason the Irish Republican Army (IRA) sought to discredit the referendum. It told Catholics to boycott the poll and they did so. Since ballots were cast almost exclusively by Protestants, a fair count showed that 98.9 per cent of those voting endorsed Northern Ireland remaining in the United Kingdom.

Legal and extra-legal military force became the primary means of resolving constitutional conflict for more than a quarter-century. The British government introduced thousands of troops to the province to restore order in the most disorderly part of the United Kingdom. Concurrently, the illegal IRA began recruiting and arming its members to defend the Catholic community and to advance its aim of Irish unity. Ulster Protestants began organizing illegal paramilitary organizations to defend the Unionist cause. In August 1971 the British Army helped implement the Northern Ireland government policy of interning without trial more than 340 Irish Catholics it suspected of supporting the IRA. In reaction, the IRA gained recruits and increased the level of violence.

The British government *stonewalled* a thorough investigation of British paratroopers killing 13 Irish nationalist demonstrators in Derry on Bloody Sunday 1972. The day after the event it set up an inquiry under Lord

Justice Widgery with narrow terms of reference. After holding hearings without visiting Derry, it concluded that those associated with the demonstration fired first and British soldiers were justified in shooting demonstrators. A group of Derry-based Irish nationalists began *chipping away* by patiently amassing and publicizing eyewitness accounts of what had happened on Bloody Sunday (Walsh 2000). In 1998 Prime Minister Tony Blair authorized a second inquiry on the grounds that it was expedient, that is, Irish Republicans made it a condition of agreeing to a peaceful settlement. On the basis of 160 volumes of evidence, in 2010 Lord Justice Saville rejected the Widgery Report and concluded that British paratroopers had fired the first shots at fleeing unarmed Irish demonstrators. Thirty-eight years after the event, Prime Minister David Cameron made a full and complete apology on behalf of the British government.

The British government began *radical institutional reform* by suspending the British-style Unionist parliament in 1972, seeking to replace it with a power-sharing government in which Unionists and Irish nationalists shared office. Initial attempts in the 1970s failed because the IRA believed a war of attrition would force the British to abandon Northern Ireland. An elected power-sharing executive was quickly brought down in 1974 by a non-violent general strike organized by Unionist workers. Northern Ireland then fell under direct rule by a British Cabinet minister; this was described as temporary but it lasted for 26 years.

Negotiating with groups previously described as terrorists became the British government policy after a quarter-century of violence had killed more than 3500 people and produced a military stalemate. The British and Unionist forces could not defeat the IRA but the IRA could not achieve Irish unification by military means. Intensive negotiations involving all parties to the conflict produced the 1998 Good Friday Agreement which mandated compulsory power-sharing and unprecedented links with the Republic of Ireland (see Chapter 6). In a referendum on the Agreement, an overwhelming majority of Catholics endorsed it as did a small majority of Protestants, producing an overall majority of 71.1 per cent. Armed violence has virtually ceased.

There is now a symptom of ill health in the conflict between the Scottish government and the Westminster government about holding a referendum on Scottish independence. The Scottish Parliament has enacted legislation authorizing a new vote. However, Downing Street claims that the government of the United Kingdom as a whole has the right to decide this. The UK government has law on its side: the 1998 Scotland Act reserved the right to call such a referendum to the Westminster Parliament. Before approving the 2014 independence referendum, the UK government got the Scottish government to agree that it would be a once-in-a-generation vote. However, the SNP has electoral legitimacy on its side: there is a commitment to an independence vote in its election manifestos. It justifies calling a new referendum on the grounds that Brexit has created a fresh situation by taking Scotland out of the European Union even though 62 per cent of referendum voters in Scotland endorsed remaining in the EU.

The absence of a written constitution makes the British body politic a toothless democracy because the courts lack the bite that courts have in the United States and the Federal Republic of Germany. From the perspective of the two governing parties, the body politic is in good health, because they can enjoy governing free of the constraints of a written constitution. The government of the day has a wide latitude to do whatever it considers necessary or politically desirable because of the hesitancy of non-elected judges to impose constraints. It can justify its actions by the constitutional doctrine of parliamentary sovereignty and by the democratic legitimacy conferred by popular election.

The absence of a written constitution means that when instances are publicized of ministers appearing to violate unwritten conventions and norms the government can be judge and jury on its own behalf. So-called independent inquiries into mistakes are not independent of the government that sets the terms of reference, appoints those who make the judgement, and can decide whether to act on an inquiry's recommendations. Even if justice is not denied, it is a symptom of ill health when justice is delayed by decades. It is also a symptom of ill health when there is a conflict about national self-determination.

References

Bradley, A.W., K.D. Ewing, and C.J.S. Knight. 2018. *Constitutional and Administrative Law*, 17th ed. Harlow: Pearson.
Chilcot, Sir John. 2016. *The Report of the Iraq Inquiry: Executive Summary.* London: House of Commons. https://gov.uk/government/uploads/system/uploads/attachment_data/file/535407/.

Cowley, Philip, and Dennis Kavanagh. 2018. *The British General Election of 2017*. London: Palgrave Macmillan.

Dicey, A.V. 1885. *The Law of the Constitution*, 2019 ed. Oxford: Oxford University Press.

Economist. 2020. Judging the Judges. *The Economist*, February 22.

Griffith, J.A.G. 1963. *Public Law*. London: Stevens.

Guardian. 2020. Letter: Ministers Must End Their Attacks on Lawyers. *The Guardian*, October 25.

Low, Sidney. 1914. *The Governance of England*. London: Benn.

Marshall, Geoffrey, and Graeme Moodie. 1959. *Some Problems of the Constitution*. London: Hutchinson.

Macrory, Patrick. 1970. *Review Body on Local Government in Northern Ireland*. Belfast: Her Majesty's Stationery Office. Cmnd. 546.

Rose, Richard. 1976. On the Priorities of Citizenship in the Deep South and Northern Ireland. *Journal of Politics* 38 (2): 247–291.

Rose, Richard. 2001. *The Prime Minister in a Shrinking World*. Oxford and Boston: Polity Press.

Stevens, Robert. 2003. *The English Judges: Their Role in the Changing Constitution*, rev. ed. Oxford: Hart.

Walsh, Dermot. 2000. *Bloody Sunday and the Rule of Law in Northern Ireland*. London: Palgrave Macmillan.

Wass, Douglas. 1986. Foreword. In Ian Harden and Norman Lewis, *The Noble Lie: The British Constitution and the Rule of Law*, viii–xiii. London: Hutchinson.

CHAPTER 8

Limits on Democratic Sovereignty

The democratic principle that the government should do what the people want is consistent with the theory that parliamentary sovereignty gives the government the power to do what it wants, such as delegating governance to other institutions or withdrawing delegated powers. However, Northern Ireland's Good Friday Agreement demonstrates the limits of parliamentary sovereignty; its terms were dictated by the need to gain acceptance by political and paramilitary groups that did not recognize the sovereignty of the UK Parliament. The Brexit movement sought to take back control over public policies that the United Kingdom had ceded to the European Union. Nonetheless, the agreements that Boris Johnson negotiated with the EU leave British individuals and firms subject to EU rules when they want to trade with or travel to Europe.

Sovereignty is an abstraction; the power implicit in the concept depends on the extent to which the Westminster government can carry out policies free of being limited by what other institutions do. However, the way government policies are delivered at the grassroots creates interdependencies that limit Westminster's sovereignty. Many policies authorized by Acts of Parliament are not delivered by Whitehall ministries. Some policies are delivered by local and devolved governments; others are in the hands of government agencies headed by professional experts and administrators; and others are delivered by private sector institutions.

R. Rose, *How Sick Is British Democracy?*
Challenges to Democracy in the 21st Century,
https://doi.org/10.1007/978-3-030-73123-6_8

Each has its own procedures and priorities. Many policy outputs combine the influence of what is decided in Whitehall and what is done by those who deliver public services.

Because foreign policy is about relations between sovereign states, this places limits on all governments when pursuing their interests through international relations. The effectiveness of British foreign policy does not depend solely on decisions taken in Westminster. Many nominally domestic policies about the economy and national security are intermestic, that is, the outcome depends on what happens internationally as well as domestically. Brexit simultaneously expanded the United Kingdom's formal sovereignty while making continued trade with the United Kingdom's biggest export market dependent on terms of trade that satisfy EU institutions. The achievement of the Brexiters' vision of a global Britain is likewise limited by the willingness of sovereign governments from Washington to Beijing to share that vision.

The mental health of the British body politic depends on how policymakers handle the cognitive dissonance between the idea of sovereignty, which implies its decisions are implemented as intended, and the limits arising when the implementation of a policy depends on what other institutions do too. Domestically, the UK government can invoke its electoral legitimacy to impose financial or legal sanctions on British institutions that do not comply with its directions. However, the success of foreign policies reflects the United Kingdom's relative power and shared interests with other countries, undemocratic as well as democratic. It is a sign of good mental health if British makers of foreign policy recognize the national interests of other countries as well as those of the United Kingdom. It is a sign of mental ill health when British politicians promote a domestically oriented foreign policy, assuming that other countries will agree without question to policies designed to promote British interests.

8.1   GOVERNANCE CREATES INTERDEPENDENCE

Governance is the process of delivering public policies to individuals, households, and private and voluntary enterprises throughout the United Kingdom. The process varies from policy to policy. There are interdependencies between services concentrated exclusively in Whitehall ministries, such as the Foreign Office and Defence. By contrast, social policies affecting millions of people must be delivered wherever people entitled to receive them live, and five-sixths of Britons do not live within a tube ride of Westminster. The delivery of health and education services is in the hands of many geographically and functionally dispersed institutions, but the payment of unemployment benefits is kept in the hands of the ministry and its own branch offices. The delivery of services within a locality is divided functionally, because specific services require different skills and qualifications. There are also interdependencies; for example, the people dealt with by social workers may also be in contact with the health service, local benefits officers or the police.

When governance involves the interdependence of Westminster and other institutions, influence is reciprocal. The relative importance of decisions made in Whitehall and elsewhere differs between policies. The treatment of a patient is primarily decided in a doctor's surgery, whereas calculations about how much income tax an individual should pay are made by computers of Her Majesty's Revenue and Customs.

As Fig. 8.1 shows, Westminster takes the initial decisions about what ought to be done. The power to make laws is concentrated there, but how laws are enforced is decided by the police and by regulators and inspectors on the ground. The minister for education sets goals for what pupils

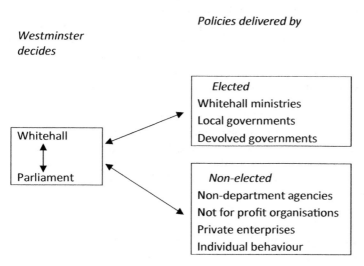

Fig. 8.1 Functional interdependence in delivering policies (*Source* Author's discussion in text)

ought to be taught, but what they actually learn is decided in the class-room and by how pupils study. Decisions about the value of pensions are taken in Whitehall but the money is distributed by departmental computers in Newcastle, and how the money is spent is decided by 12 million pensioners. Of the 5.4 million Britons in public employment, less than one-tenth are civil servants employed by Whitehall departments and only one-tenth of 1 per cent are civil servants influencing public policy. The great bulk are not faceless bureaucrats; they are familiar faces in the communities in which they work as teachers, nurses or police.

Interdependence between electoral constituencies. Each newly elected government is limited by the legacy of programmes established by their Labour and Conservative predecessors. The legacy includes laws that specify what the minister must and can do and spending commitments that leave little money to fund new initiatives (Rose and Davies 1994). This legacy limits the capacity of a minister to launch new initiatives and pressure groups can mobilize opposition to any new ministerial initiative that they see as harmful to their interests. For example, the Police Federation can lobby against any proposal by a Home Secretary to restrict the powers of the police and the National Farmers Union can lobby to prevent any reduction in agricultural subsidies.

Even though the governing party is collectively accountable to the electorate, agreement on policies is limited by departments with overlapping interests pushing against each other. The annual public expenditure cycle is an example of interdepartmental interdependence. Whatever the merits of a single department's claim for increased expenditure, there is a limit to the total amount of money that the Chancellor has available for increasing public expenditure without a politically unacceptable increase in taxes or the public deficit. For Joel Barnett, a Labour Treasury minister, the aim was to win three-quarters of public spending negotiations with other Cabinet ministers: 'If we won only half the disputes we'd destroy the Treasury, and if we won all of them we'd destroy the Labour government'.

Every elector casts a vote in at least two constituencies, one for the Westminster Parliament and the other for local government. Residents in Scotland, Wales and Northern Ireland elect devolved parliaments too. Elections are separately timed because MPs do not want their own contest to compete with or be confused by contests for other offices. In consequence, democratically accountable political institutions responsible for delivering a given policy may be controlled by politicians representing competing parties.

There is functional interdependence between Whitehall departments that decide the terms and finance of public policies and local authorities that deliver them. Because both local councillors and government ministers are elected, this creates the potential for democratic friction. Councillors can argue that local people know best, while ministers can claim to represent the national interest. Moreover, local councils controlled by parties that are in opposition at Westminster often have different political priorities than the government of the day. At present the Conservatives control 170 local councils, less than half of Britain's total of 393 councils. Whichever party is in control in Westminster, friction is especially likely with nationalist parties controlling devolved governments in Scotland and Northern Ireland.

Friction arises too from the tendency of Westminster to give locally elected institutions more policy responsibilities than money. Thus, local councillors can blame Westminster for having to make cuts in local standards, and the central government can blame local governments that do not meet the national standards it sets. In Scotland and Northern Ireland nationalist parties can argue that independence would reduce the friction arising from interdependence, while ignoring that this would put paid to the financial subsidies devolved governments receive from the UK Treasury.

Governance beyond elected governors. The legitimacy conferred by election is necessary for democratic governance, but it is not sufficient. To deliver many of its policies, Whitehall depends on people with the expertise to do the job. The delivery of health services requires the professional skills of doctors, nurses and X-ray technicians and a host of other technical skills rarely found among democratically elected politicians in Westminster. Even though these professionals deliver public policies in the public interest, they consider themselves non-political because their agencies are not headed by politicians accountable to the electorate. Nonetheless, they are accountable to the National Audit Office for the money that they receive from the Treasury, and MPs can question agency heads as well as the minister who gives them direction.

Non-departmental public agencies have the expert knowledge necessary to deliver policies effectively. By being free of civil service commitments such as permanent employment and pensions, they may cost less taxpayers' money than civil servants employed in Whitehall. However, insofar as Whitehall contracts with profit-making firms to keep costs down while private enterprises want to keep profits up, false economies can result if standards of service deteriorate.

Outsourcing limits the capacity of Whitehall departments to determine policy outputs for which they are accountable to the electorate. The coronavirus statistics that government ministers produce on television to justify their policies are the aggregated results of actions of health care workers. The training of doctors focuses on how to diagnose and meet the needs of individual patients for treatment. This is very different from the Ministry of Health priority of getting good statistics about health care. In short-staffed hospitals and surgeries, doctors may decide to let queues of non-urgent patients lengthen, to the political embarrassment of ministers, rather than short-change patients by cursory examination and treatment.

The behaviour of individuals places limits on public policy that are far greater than electoral accountability. The health of the population is determined by how individuals look after themselves as well as by how the National Health Service treats the consequences of individual choices. The success of government policy to reduce obesity depends on millions of adults and children changing what they eat. Neither governing party has shown an appetite to adopt laws banning, heavily taxing or rationing fattening foods that individuals buy. Instead, policymakers have turned to exhortation and education in efforts to stimulate people to choose a healthy diet.

The achievement of targets for the national economy is outsourced to the marketplace. For example, the minister for housing can set a target for the number of houses to be built in a year, but achieving the target depends on what house-builders do. Because builders are motivated by profit, the number of houses they build each year goes up and down with the demand from buyers. The number of buyers for new houses is limited by household income and the cost of a monthly mortgage. The law that determines the achievement of a government housing target is not an Act of Parliament but the law of supply and demand.

In an effort to control outsourced policies for which they remain accountable, Whitehall departments set quantitative targets that extra-Whitehall bodies are expected to meet, such as the percentage of pupils passing mathematics examinations or the length of time people must wait for treatment in hospital accident and emergency queues. Setting targets is consistent with the minister's political legitimacy, while leaving professionals free to decide how to achieve them. It also creates an incentive for agencies to focus on producing target indicators regardless of the effect on the treatment of pupils or emergency patients (Boswell 2018). A classic example of distortion is the readiness of the police to meet a target of clearing up crimes by not recording minor offences that are reported to them.

By outsourcing services, ministers distance themselves from being immediately accountable for taking decisions. Ministers can still take credit for successful actions by an outsourced agency while shifting blame to the agency for an unsuccessful policy. For example, ministers blame leading universities for the low proportion of youths they admit from poor and disadvantaged backgrounds rather than blaming this on the failure of the schools for which ministers are responsible to educate pupils to the standard required to secure a good university place.

The limitations that interdependence imposes on Westminster are the inevitable result of policies being delivered by institutions accountable to different electorates or outsourced to one or another type of specialist institution. For example, the secretary of state for Education heads a department that, according to its website, is concerned with 27 different services affecting young people, ranging from adoption to vocational education. A few are delivered by the ministry's own staff or other Whitehall departments, some by local authorities and others by non-departmental public agencies, profit-making firms or not-for-profit institutions such as universities.

Governance is in good democratic health when these differences can be resolved by bargaining. This is most readily realized when the collective responsibility of the government of the day to the electorate makes departmental ministers resolve their differences, if necessary by the intervention of Downing Street. It is likewise healthy for democracy when differences between the nationally elected central government and locally elected council authorities can be settled by bargaining. If a dispute persists, ministers can claim greater legitimacy to make a decision because they are accountable to the entire UK electorate. If the interactions involve so many diverse institutions that negotiation is not feasible, then government ministers are subject to the verdict of the American cartoon character Pogo: We have met the enemy and they are us.

8.2   No Island Is an Island unto Itself

National sovereignty and winning an election do not insulate a democratically elected government from the limitations of interdependence. The British government cannot advance the country's national security by a policy of national isolation. For military defence, the United Kingdom relies on membership in NATO and its nominally independent nuclear weapons are dependent on American technology. Combatting terrorism requires dealing with its trans-national causes. Because sterling remains a major global currency, its international value depends not only on Bank of England decisions but also on dealings in foreign exchange markets around the globe. As former prime minister John Major told a BBC interviewer during the 2016 referendum campaign: 'If you want undiluted sovereignty in the modern age when everybody is interconnected, then go to North Korea because that's where you will get it'.

The changing terms of interdependence. The first steps towards a global Britain occurred centuries before it became democratic. The country's island status encouraged the development of sea power linking Britain with other continents and distanced it from the land-based powers of continental Europe. Winston Churchill claimed Britain was a unique world power because it was part of three circles of global importance: the Empire, Europe and an Anglo-American world based in Washington. The special relationship with Washington came first. The 1945–1951 Labour government gave priority to securing an American guarantee to the military defence of the United Kingdom through the creation of NATO. Prime Minister Harold Macmillan saw interdependence with the United States as extending Britain's influence: 'These Americans represent the new Roman empire and we Britons, like the Greeks of old, must teach them how to make it go' (quoted in Hitchens 2006).

The legacy of Britain's global pre-eminence has encouraged unhealthy misperceptions of the United Kingdom's place in a world that is now very different from what it was three-quarters of a century ago. In 1949 the chief science adviser to the Ministry of Defence, Sir Henry Tizard, warned that Britain was 'not a great power and never will be again. We are a great nation, but if we continue to behave like a great power we shall soon cease to be a great nation' (quoted in Young 1998: 24). British prime ministers from Thatcher to Blair and Boris Johnson have preferred to follow Churchill rather than Tizard. Iain Duncan Smith, a former Conservative party leader, has gone so far as describing Brexit as offering young Britons the opportunity to dominate the world again.

Since Winston Churchill left Downing Street in 1954, Britain's national economy has quadrupled in real terms and democracy has not been challenged by the equivalent of Donald Trump. Nonetheless, Britain's global position has undergone relative decline as new powers have emerged on the global scene. The People's Republic of China is now a military and economic superpower, and Germany and Japan have recovered from military defeat to become major powers; the gross domestic product of India is now similar to that of Britain. The trajectory of the pound charts Britain's relative decline in the world. When Churchill left office, the pound was worth $4.20 or 11 German Deutsch Marks in foreign exchange markets. At the beginning of 2021, it was worth two-thirds less against the dollar and had fallen by almost nine-tenths against Germany's successor currency, the euro.

The United Kingdom is no longer one of the world's greatest powers: the People's Republic of China and the European Union have replaced it. The population of China is more than twenty times larger than Britain's, the European Union is more than six times larger, and the United States five times more populous. The gross domestic product of the American economy is seven times that of Britain, and the European Union and China are each five times larger. Britain accounts for only 3 per cent of world trade.

Figure 8.2 illustrates how the position of the United Kingdom is no longer central in international affairs. It remains distinctive in having a

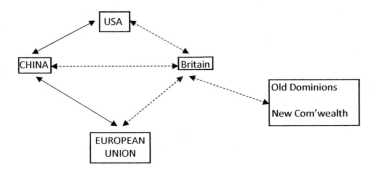

Fig. 8.2 Britain's place in the world today (*Source* Author's discussion in text)

link with Old Dominions and the New Commonwealth, but it is not a link that is highly valued by the world's three greatest powers. A special relationship with the United States still exists but it is not so special as Washington's link with China. While the United Kingdom was engaging in weakening its relationship with the European Union, the EU was negotiating a stronger trade link with China. In Hong Kong, China has demonstrated its disregard for commitments made to the United Kingdom before taking over this former British territory.

The British public tends to accept interdependence as a fact of life. When people are asked whether Britain should be open to the rest of the world or give priority to protecting the country from global influences, only 23 per cent give priority to treating the country's island status as a moat isolating it from the rest of the world. Moreover, people tend to view positively the influence of other countries on Britain's economy and on their own lives. On average only 17 per cent think other countries have a negative influence. People who see the impact of other countries in positive terms outnumber those who are negative by margins of up to three to one (Ipsos MORI 2019: 22, 29).

Given interdependence, the critical question is whether the government can make more effective intermestic policies by co-operating with others or by doing things on its own. Four months before the Brexit referendum, a BMG survey asked whether Britain could count on others when dealing with problems of the global economy, immigration, terrorism and military threats (Rose 2020: Table 10.1). It offered as allies the United Nations, the EU or the United States. A total of 59 per cent said Britain needed to look after immigration by itself and 46 per cent said the same about dealing with problems in the national economy. While pluralities thought Britain should work with others to deal with terrorism and military threats, there was no agreement about where to turn. To deal with military threats, 26 per cent favoured help from the UN, 20 per cent the United States and 8 per cent the EU. There was a similar division of opinion about which way the British government should turn for assistance in dealing with terrorism.

Managing interdependence. The prime minister is responsible for representing the UK in foreign affairs. The prime minister discusses issues with leaders of other governments in phone calls, meets heads of government visiting London, and networks at meetings of international organizations such as the United Nations. A small team of civil servants in Downing Street supports the prime minister's international role. Three of Britain's five most recent prime ministers have entered Downing Street with no experience of conducting Britain's foreign affairs, and Boris Johnson's brief tenure as Foreign Secretary showed the priority he gave to domestic politics. While being responsible for foreign policy makes the prime minister an international figure it also makes him or her accountable nationally for the consequences of interdependent policies that Britain may influence but not control.

Intermestic policies place greater or lesser limitations on major Whitehall departments. The success or failure of three Whitehall departments—the Foreign, Commonwealth and Development Office, Defence and Trade—inevitably depends on the policies of other governments. The impact of the global economy on the British economy requires the Treasury to take account of it when making British economic policy. The Home Office's responsibility for legal and illegal immigration is only one of its many concerns, but it is also one of the government's most politically sensitive issues. Most Whitehall departments are selectively concerned with what happens outside the United Kingdom. For example, the road and rail responsibilities of the Department of Transport focus on travel within Britain, while the bulk of air travel is between British airports and foreign destinations.

Insofar as common problems create common interests, measures can be developed through intergovernmental institutions. The British government is a founder member of the United Nations, the International Monetary Fund and the World Bank. It also belongs to more than 100 lesser organizations such as the International Whaling Commission. Membership gives Whitehall departments contacts with public officials dealing with similar problems in other countries, and a forum for exchanging ideas and, as appropriate, the development of common practices and standards. The cost of joining is usually low and the political cost is lower still. Unlike the binding commitments of the European Union, the policies of international organizations are usually statements of goals. Member governments are free to decide for themselves whether to adopt their recommendations as national policies.

The British government has well over a hundred embassies abroad to put forward its views on major issues and to feed back to London information and insights about other countries. Whitehall ministries dealing with major intermestic issues post staff abroad to liaise with their foreign counterparts. For example, in the British Embassy in Washington, DC, less than half its 460 staff are Foreign Office diplomats. British military and security staff liaise with the Pentagon and the CIA, and Treasury staff link with the IMF and World Bank as well as networking with the Federal Reserve Bank and the US Treasury.

The emergence of English as the dominant language of international communication gives the United Kingdom a form of soft power, a global network of people who, in the course of becoming proficient in English, have incidentally become familiar with Britain. Moreover, foreigners usually prefer to learn to speak English rather than American. English as a second language is spoken globally by more than ten times the population of the United Kingdom. It is a soft power asset because it creates greater and broader knowledge of Britain than foreigners are likely to have of France or Germany. The 165 foreign embassies and missions in London are usually staffed by high-status diplomats. They have soft power too. Years of studying English and the English tend to make them better informed about the politics of Britain than British politicians are about their country (Rose 2008). Foreigners not only talk to official sources but also follow British politics through the *Economist*, the *Financial Times*, the *Weekly Guardian* and the BBC World Service.

In a world in which undemocratic countries are powerful, the healthiness of British foreign policy cannot be evaluated by domestic democratic standards. It is more appropriate to evaluate it in terms of the realism with which a government promotes its interests. Statements by prime ministers that Britain can punch at the same weight internationally as it did in 1945 are a symptom of cognitive impairment. As John Major said in November 2020, 'We are no longer a great power. We will never be so again. We are a top second-rank power'. Ignoring interdependence in the misplaced belief that nominal sovereignty insulates Britain's public policies from external influences means that, when actions of foreign governments have an unhealthy domestic British impact, this comes as an unwelcome surprise.

8.3   Brexit: A Domestic Foreign Policy

The campaign to withdraw the United Kingdom from the European Union had as its goal taking back control of British public policies from Brussels. In the words of Lord Frost, Britain's chief negotiator of withdrawal for Boris Johnson, 'We believe sovereignty is meaningful and what it enables us to do is to set our rules for our own benefit' (Parker et al. 2021). However, the United Kingdom's withdrawal from the European

Union has not ended the interdependence of the EU and Britain. The immediate effect has been to create a different set of interdependencies. The United Kingdom's freedom from EU regulations as a member state has been replaced by being subject to EU rules applying to countries that are not member states. The United Kingdom is now free to make new trade agreements with countries on other continents, but doing so depends on accepting conditions laid down in Washington and Beijing and not just in Westminster.

Europe as a domestic policy. When European governments committed themselves to political and economic integration in the 1950s, the Conservative government of the day rejected partnership as economically unnecessary and politically undesirable. The Labour leader, Hugh Gaitskell, told the 1962 Labour party conference that joining the EU would mean 'the end of a thousand years of history' by making Britain a province of Europe.

When Britain did join what politicians called the Common Market, the case for doing so was presented as benefiting the domestic economy. Enoch Powell and Tony Benn opposed membership on political grounds: the obligations of membership infringed Britain's sovereignty. In a television address in 1973, Prime Minister Edward Heath rejected this view: 'There are some in this country who fear that, in going into Europe, we shall in some way sacrifice independence and sovereignty. These fears, I need hardly say, are completely unjustified'. Advocates of Common Market membership argued that any expansion of its powers would occur as a result of British leadership in promoting policies in Britain's national interest. This was the initial view of Prime Minister Margaret Thatcher, who successfully promoted the introduction of the European Single Market.

Party leaders did not see Europe as an issue that would win votes and, given divisions within both parties, discussing the issue would only stimulate intra-party quarrels. When the EU adopted policies furthering European integration such as the replacement of national currencies with the euro, the British government opted out. When polls asked about support for membership, there was a three-way division between those in favour, opposed, and without any opinion; over the decades each was sometimes the largest group (Westlake 2020).

The timing of the 2016 referendum on EU membership reflected the domestic electoral pressure of the United Kingdom Independence Party (UKIP) on the Conservative government. The campaign to remain in the EU emphasized the cost to the national economy and to the average household of leaving the European Union. It avoided discussing the political requirements of membership. The Leave campaign, by contrast, called for restoring British sovereignty by taking back control from Brussels. Boris Johnson was photographed by the side of a bus that showed the claim, 'We send the EU £350 million a week, let's fund our NHS instead'. When challenged two years later, Johnson claimed the figure was an underestimate.

The referendum result showed an unhealthy division between MPs who favoured remaining in the EU and a majority of voters who did not. A Press Association survey found that 75 per cent of MPs said they would vote remain, consistent with the bipartisan support that the House of Commons had always given EU membership. This was half again greater than the 48.1 per cent of voters who endorsed remaining in the EU. Whereas fewer than half the Conservative MPs voted to leave, a substantial majority of Conservative voters did so. Labour MPs were half again more likely to vote for remaining in the EU than were Labour voters. Labour MPs who favoured the EU felt tension when it appeared that their constituency vote had favoured Brexit (Clarke et al. 2017).

Foreigners place limits on implementing Brexit. Article 50 of the Treaty on European Union recognized the sovereign right of any member state to withdraw from the EU in accordance with its own constitutional arrangements. It also set out conditions for the EU negotiating the terms of withdrawal and future relations. Once the United Kingdom withdrawal was notified in March 2017, Downing Street learned the hard way that the European Union was anxious to maintain its sovereignty too.

Within hours of the referendum result becoming known, European Union leaders began preparing a strategy to defend its unique form of multi-national sovereignty against the impact of Britain's withdrawal (Van Middelaar 2019; Rose 2020: 184ff.). The overriding principle was to protect the EU's political authority in relation to its 27 member states and the European Single Market. These goals meant that the United Kingdom, as a non-member state, could not enjoy the full range of economic and social benefits of member states; in order to receive any benefits the United Kingdom would have to conform to obligations applicable to member states. The EU saw Britain as needing a trade deal more than it did: 43 per cent of UK exports went to EU member states in 2019, while the United Kingdom accounted for only 6 per cent of the EU's exports.

The European Commission was designated the sole EU institution for negotiating with the UK government to prevent the UK from trying to put pressure on Brussels by lobbying national governments of member states. The Commission is unique in its staff being committed exclusively to the supra-national Commission, unlike nationally elected Members of the European Parliament and national politicians meeting in the European Council. Commission staff are very experienced in conducting trade negotiations whereas the United Kingdom was short-staffed, since Whitehall had not had experience in negotiating trade deals since before the United Kingdom joined the European Union in 1973.

The British advocates of Brexit had campaigned for a simple principle, withdrawal from the European Union. They were as optimistic as they were unprepared for the task of negotiating future relations with Britain's biggest trading partner. The Brexit secretary David Davis tweeted, 'There will be no downside to Brexit, only a considerable upside'. The International Trade minister Liam Fox predicted that the task of negotiating a free-trade agreement with the EU would be 'one of the easiest in history'. Boris Johnson, then Foreign Secretary, told *The Sun*, 'Our policy is to have our cake and eat it'.

The domestic politics of the Conservative parliamentary party was of first importance to Prime Minister Theresa May. To reassure pro-Brexit MPs, she declared that no deal would be better than a deal that allowed the EU to enforce its rules on Britain in exchange for giving Britain access to the European Single Market. Negotiations with Brussels quickly showed May that she could only secure trade benefits by accepting EU obligations unacceptable to many Conservative MPs. After deciding the consequences of no deal were unsatisfactory, in November 2018 May agreed terms for Britain's EU divorce. The agreement was three times rejected by the House of Commons (see Chapter 3). Having failed to bridge the gap between domestic and foreign policy imperatives, in May 2019 Theresa May resigned as prime minister.

When Boris Johnson became prime minister he put domestic politics first: his overriding political goal was to get Brexit done on terms that respected British sovereignty (Parker et al. 2021). As the climax of negotiations approached in December 2020, the chief EU negotiator, Michel Barnier, tweeted, 'We respect the sovereignty of the UK and we expect the same'. To defend British sovereignty, Johnson rejected seeking retention of EU benefits enjoyed by diverse groups such as undergraduates studying on Erasmus, road hauliers, and the City of London because it would require accepting EU regulation of their cross-border activities. Johnson repeatedly asserted that, rather than accept terms that infringed British sovereignty, the United Kingdom would leave with no deal; he dismissed as irrelevant or speculative calculations of the economic costs of his priorities.

The outcome. The negotiations confirming Britain's future relations with the European Union demonstrated the limits of British sovereignty. Although two of the three points in the Withdrawal Agreement—a financial payment and the status of EU citizens resident in Britain and British citizens living in the EU—did not raise issues of sovereignty, the treatment of Northern Ireland did. It introduced a novel economic border within the United Kingdom between Great Britain and Northern Ireland so that the latter could trade with the Republic of Ireland as if it were part of the EU. Johnson's December 2019 election victory enabled the Withdrawal Agreement to be confirmed by the new Parliament with no questions asked. However, Johnson tacitly accepted that the Agreement infringed British sovereignty by subsequently introducing an Internal Market bill with a clause authorizing the British government to administer trade with Northern Ireland on terms that violated the Withdrawal Agreement. When this became a stumbling block in negotiating future terms of trade with the EU, it was quietly withdrawn.

A Trade and Co-operation Agreement (TCA) was reached with the EU on 24 December, only a week before transition arrangements were due to expire, leaving the United Kingdom with no deal with its biggest trade partner. The Agreement was presented to Parliament on 30 December 2020 on a take-it-or-leave-it basis. Confronted with the choice between confirming the Agreement and no deal, both the Commons and the Lords gave their approval without question in a single sitting.

The TCA was cosmetically designed to allow both sides to claim they had achieved their political goals. Boris Johnson boasted, 'We have taken back control of our money, borders, laws, trade and our fishing waters'. Instead of being subject to conditions specified in EU laws and EU regulations, the United Kingdom is now subject to conditions set out in the 1286 pages of the Trade and Co-operation Agreement. Instead of the European Court of Justice having jurisdiction, special arrangements have been established for arbitration, and the EU has the unilateral power to suspend commercial benefits if it deems the United Kingdom is defaulting on its obligation to maintain economic and employment regulations equivalent to EU standards. Trade in manufactured and agricultural goods, in which the EU has a surplus with the United Kingdom, is free of tariffs and customs, but the TCA does not cover trade in services, in which the UK has had a surplus with the EU.

Democracy is in better health when Westminster is engaged in the governance of the United Kingdom than when negotiating with governments outside the United Kingdom. There is a shared purpose between Whitehall departments and institutions within the United Kingdom to which responsibilities and money are delegated to deliver policies. Because the United Kingdom is legally a unitary state, the Westminster government has the final word when differences arise between it and elected and non-elected public bodies.

The referendum majority to leave the European Union was the consequence of a persisting unhealthy relationship between British politicians and citizens about the United Kingdom's membership in the EU. Politicians did not encourage popular appreciation of Britain's engagement in European Union affairs nor did the Conservative and Labour parties mobilize supporters to vote in European Parliament elections. The United Kingdom consistently had the lowest turnout at European Parliament elections of any of the 15 older member states. Elite inactivity reflected the misplaced belief that the government's activities in EU institutions did not require mass commitment.

The low profile of foreign policy issues in general elections gives the government of the day a freer hand than it enjoys domestically. However, achieving foreign policy goals depends not only on decisions taken in Westminster but also on decisions taken by other sovereign states. British politicians accustomed to appearing all-powerful in Westminster have shown symptoms of mental ill health, failing to recognize that the United Kingdom no longer carries the weight it once did.

REFERENCES

Boswell, Cristina. 2018. *Manufacturing Political Trust: Target and Performance Measurement in Public Policy*. Cambridge: Cambridge University Press.
Clarke, Harold, M. Goodwin, and P. Whiteley. 2017. *Brexit: Why Britain Voted to Leave the European Union*. Cambridge: Cambridge University Press.
Hitchens, Christopher J. 2006. *Blood, Class and Empire: The Enduring Anglo-American Relationship*. London: Atlantic Books.

Ipsos MORI. 2019. *Global Britain*. London: UK in a Changing Europe and The Policy Institute King's College London.

Parker, George, P. Foster, S. Fleming, and J. Brunsden. 2021. How the Deal Was Built and What Happens Next. *FT Weekend Magazine*, January 23, 14–21.

Rose, Richard. 2008. Political Communication in a European Public Space. *Journal of Common Market Studies* 46 (2): 451–475.

Rose, Richard. 2020. *How Referendums Challenge European Democracy*. London: Palgrave Macmillan.

Rose, Richard, and Philip Davies. 1994. *Inheritance in Public Policy*. New Haven: Yale University Press.

Van Middelaar, Luuk. 2019. *Alarums & Excursions: Improvising Politics on the European Stage*. Newcastle upon Tyne: Agenda.

Westlake, Martin. 2020. *Slipping Loose: The UK's Long Drift Away from the European Union*. Newcastle upon Tyne: Agenda.

Young, Hugo. 1998. *This Blessed Plot: Britain and Europe from Churchill to Blair*. London: Macmillan.

CHAPTER 9

A Mixed Bill of Health for British Democracy

It is unrealistic to expect anything as complex as the body politic to be in perfect health all the time; it is also unrealistic to project symptoms of a serious problem in one institution onto all parts of the body politic. The mixture of positive and negative symptoms in the health of British democracy is normal; fluctuations are also normal. British democracy is in good health if it is resilient, that is, capable of responding positively to evidence that it is not working as it should.

Paradoxically, chronic symptoms of poor health for a quarter-century or more are not indications that British democracy is dying; persistence of a symptom shows that its effects are not fatal, for example, less than three-quarters of the registered electorate turning out to vote at a general election. The point of intermittent disturbances to political health is that they not only occur suddenly but also go away quickly. For example, the United Kingdom Independence Party (UKIP) under Nigel Farage's populist leadership quadrupled its 2010 vote to 12.6 per cent in 2015 by mobilizing support for Britain to leave the European Union. UKIP's mission accomplished by the Brexit referendum, its vote fell to 1.8 per cent in 2017 and 2.0 per cent in 2019.

The coronavirus pandemic has challenged the effectiveness of the British government; however, it has not challenged its democratic health.

© The Author(s), under exclusive license to Springer Nature Switzerland AG 2021
R. Rose, *How Sick Is British Democracy?*
Challenges to Democracy in the 21st Century,
https://doi.org/10.1007/978-3-030-73123-6_9

Government restrictions on social contact, especially at the level of total lockdown, are restrictions on freedom of association and movement unprecedented even in wartime. Like wartime restrictions, the principle of limiting individual freedom for the collective good is accepted as democratic not only by all parties in Parliament but also by citizens voluntarily complying with severe lockdown measures designed to arrest the coronavirus pandemic.

Free elections are the democratic means of institutionalizing resilience in the body politic. Elections give voters the opportunity to hold the government of the day accountable for its faults, and public opinion polls send constant signals to politicians reminding them of maladies needing a cure. After Theresa May's government and a hung Parliament could not agree about how to implement Brexit, her successor, Boris Johnson, called an election that gave the Conservative government the absolute majority needed to get Brexit done. At the next general election the electorate can hold the government accountable for the way it has handled Brexit, the coronavirus pandemic and much else. If Conservative MPs become anxious that they may lose the election, they can hold Boris Johnson accountable and install a new prime minister in hopes he or she will reverse their electoral fortune.

Patients go to a doctor hoping that, however their symptoms are diagnosed, the doctor can prescribe either a cure, such as surgery, or pills to manage a persisting illness. The next section shows that most citizens see British democracy as in need of treatment for ill health. The diagnosis that follows identifies specific symptoms of political ill health that are amenable to treatment by institutional reform; others that are chronic conditions that must be lived with; and considers whether there is any evidence of fatal symptoms.

9.1   What Britons Think of Democracy

Since democracy is about government on behalf of the people, the views of the mass of the British people ought to be relevant. However, the peaceful and uninterrupted evolution of democracy in Britain means that people have not needed to think about democracy: it is taken for granted. Nonetheless, a lifetime of experiencing democratic governance does not breed indifference to democracy as an ideal. When asked for their views about the importance of different features of democracy, on average only 6 per cent of Britons replied don't know in the European Social Survey

(ESS). An overwhelming majority consistently endorse all the institutional characteristics of the democratic ideal (Fig. 9.1). The chief difference among respondents is the proportion of people who give the practice of particular institutions 10 marks out of 10 and those giving marks just below the top. The ideal characteristics rated the highest are government following the rule of law, holding free elections, and explaining its decisions to citizens.

Consistent with the body politic having a mixed bill of health, Britons tend to discriminate in assessing how well the country's political institutions work in reality. The highest positive ratings are given to the working of free elections and freedom to criticize the government of the day. They are almost as highly regarded in practice as their importance is rated in the abstract (Fig. 9.1). By contrast, the way in which the government explains to citizens what it is doing receives the least favourable

Ideal: *How important do you think it is for democracy in general that..?*
(Not at all: 0. Extremely important: (10).
Reality: *To what extent do you think the following statements apply in Britain (Not at all: 0.*
Applies completely: 10).

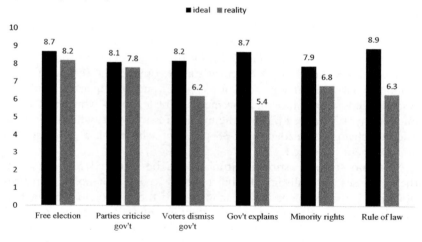

Fig. 9.1 Democracy as an ideal and in reality (*Source* British respondents in Sixth European Social Survey, as reported in Monica Ferrin and Hanspeter Kriesi, ed., *How Europeans View and Evaluate Democracy.* Oxford: Oxford University Press, 2016, Tables A, 3.1, 8.1)

rating, 5.4, midway between a very positive and very negative rating. Relatively less favourable ratings for performance are also given to the ability of voters to dismiss the government; this may reflect the fact that at general elections well over half of British voters endorse one or another Opposition party.

Although all six democratic practices are rated positively, there are significant gaps between the ideal and the practice of British democracy on four criteria. The gap is 3.3 points out of 10 for the way the government explains what it is doing to voters; 2.6 points for following the rule of law; and 2.0 points between the importance of voters being able to dismiss the government and how this works in practice.

Much has happened in British politics since the fieldwork for the European Social Survey was undertaken in 2012. Events are unlikely to cause people to change their views of democratic ideals, but their evaluation of how democracy works in practice may fluctuate with events such as the Brexit referendum and its consequences. The endorsement of democracy as an ideal remains high. When YouGov asked Britons in September 2020 their view of democracy as a way of governing a country, 78 per cent gave a positive reply compared to 11 per cent having no opinion and 11 per cent being negative.

Popular awareness of the less-than-ideal state of democratic practice is complemented by public endorsement of the need to improve the workings of British democracy (Fig. 9.2). Of the respondents to the Hansard Society's 2019 Audit of Democracy survey, only 2 per cent think it is working well without any need for change, and one-quarter think the system needs only minor improvements. The majority who think more improvement is needed include the median respondents, who think quite a lot of change is needed, and 38 per cent who think a great deal of improvement is needed.

Since no set of existing institutions can be expected to be perfect, the responses are realistic. The big majority saying that political institutions need improvement is similar in size to the proportion saying that British political institutions to some extent live up to democratic ideals (cf. Figs. 9.1 and 9.2). This suggests that the desire for improvement comes from people who already view democratic institutions positively rather than from people who are strongly dissatisfied and might even welcome their replacement by undemocratic institutions. The desire for reform rather than getting rid of democracy is also evident in fascist and revolutionary Marxist parties getting less than one-hundredth of 1 per cent of

Q. Which statement best describes your opinion on the present system governing Britain?

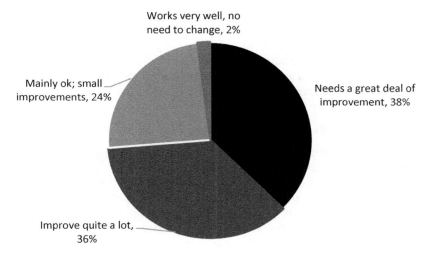

Fig. 9.2 How much improvement is needed in Britain's democracy? (*Source* Hansard Society, Audit of Political Engagement 16 (London: Hansard Society, 2019), p. 42. Survey by Ipsos-MORI of 1198 respondents, 30 November–12 December 2018. Three per cent of don't knows excluded)

the vote for the handful of candidates that they sometimes nominate at British general elections.

There has been an increase of 12 percentage points since 2004 in the size of the majority thinking that British political institutions need a great deal or quite a lot of improvement. The increase started with the scandal about MPs' expenses in 2009 and rose a few points more as the government and Parliament struggled to decide what Brexit meant. The persistence of the desire for improvement under both Labour and Conservative governments suggests that, although people see free elections working well, more than a change between a Conservative and Labour government is needed in order to achieve a major improvement in the health of the democratic body politic.

9.2   DIAGNOSIS: INTERMITTENT ILLS, NONE FATAL

The institutions of a healthy democracy have three critical functions: citizens must have an opportunity to choose the government of the day; governors must be able to give direction to government; and periodic elections must give voters the means of holding the government accountable. The detailed examination of the functioning of the British body politic in the past quarter-century finds symptoms indicating that parts of its anatomy are intermittently or chronically sick.

9.2.1   Representation Healthy, Problems Intermittent

The electoral system that is at the heart of British democracy is in good health. The first-past-the-post system does what it is intended to do. By focusing on a choice between two parties competing for control of government, voters can clearly hold the winning party accountable for its actions at the following general election. Public authorities annually update the register of the electorate, it is easy for candidates to get on the ballot, competing parties can nominate poll-watchers, and votes are counted under the scrutiny of all candidates and their supporters. If a constituency result is very close, the losing candidate can demand a recount, thus forestalling subsequent allegations of fraud. Moreover, if a winning candidate in a single constituency should be disqualified, for example, for breaking spending limits, this would not affect which party has control of the government.

The majority of voters now have the psychological freedom to choose between parties in the light of their current views rather than family legacies (cf. Butler and Stokes 1969). Studies of voting behaviour describe this as a shock destabilizing the party system (Fieldhouse et al. 2020). However, in terms of democratic theory, contemporary voters making their choice of party free of the influence of parents and class is a positive sign. It also strengthens the accountability of the governing party to the electorate. Party leaders introduce major changes in their party to take into account changes in their electoral support. For example, Tony Blair created a New Labour appeal to win more votes from an increasingly middle-class electorate, and David Cameron made it his mission to 'de-toxify' the Conservative party by endorsing twenty-first-century values.

In two of seven elections since 1997, the electoral system has failed to give a parliamentary majority to the party winning the most seats. The consequences have shown the resilience of the governing parties. In 2010 the Liberal Democrats won 23 per cent of the vote and 57 MPs, leading to the first peacetime coalition government since 1931. In the following election, the electorate reacted against coalition; the Liberal Democrats' vote fell by almost two-thirds and the Conservatives won an absolute majority in Parliament. At the 2017 general election, the combined vote for the two governing parties rose to 82.3 per cent and the Conservatives were forced to form the first minority government since 1974. In reaction to the indecisiveness that resulted (see Chapter 3), the Conservative party won a big majority at the 2019 election.

The decentralized nomination of parliamentary candidates by 650 local constituency parties has a healthy effect on the social diversity of the House of Commons. In the past quarter-century Labour and Conservative constituency parties in safe seats have nominated many women, black, Asian and minority ethnic (BAME) candidates in significant numbers. This has created a presence in the House of Commons of MPs who represent the social diversity of British society today. In Margaret Thatcher's first Cabinet all members were White men except for herself. In Tony Blair's first Cabinet there were five women but no BAME ministers. In the Cabinet that Boris Johnson formed after winning the 2019 election more than one-third of ministers were women, from an ethnic minority, or both. However, in social class all parties are unrepresentative of their voters. More than three-quarters of MPs are university graduates compared with a limited minority of the electorate. Hardly any MPs come from the manual working class, still a substantial part of the electorate. However, the effect on political health is limited because of the weak link between class and political values today and the fairly close alignment of political and economic attitudes of party leaders and their voters (see Tables 3.2 and 3.3).

Party discipline in the House of Commons has a positive effect on political accountability. Whatever their social characteristics or personal views on issues, Conservative and Labour MPs usually follow the instructions of their party whips when divisions are called in the House of Commons. MPs can individually abstain or even vote against the party whip on an issue as long as they do not form a group large enough to threaten the governing party's majority. The disciplined support that MPs in the majority party give the government is good for democratic account-ability because it gives voters the certainty that whichever parliamentary candidate they favour in their constituency, their choice will support a Conservative or Labour government.

The system that parties use to choose their leader and potential prime minister is intermittently healthy. In a healthy system of party govern-ment, a party leader should be good at winning votes and at giving direction to the government. Internal party reforms that removed the right of MPs to choose the leader have weakened the capacity of the party to choose an effective prime minister. Giving party members the final say in the choice of party leader favours the candidate most popular with members. The change was justified as democratizing the party. However, this is a very restrictive form of democratization, because party members are less than 5 per cent of the people who vote for the party at a general election. It is also ineffective in picking election winners. Seven of the 10 party leaders chosen after party members were given a decisive vote have never won a general election.

Conservative MPs have demonstrated a healthy willingness to push out of Downing Street a leader who is performing badly in government and opinion polls. This was most strikingly demonstrated in 1990 when Margaret Thatcher failed to win a vote of confidence of Conservative MPs and resigned as prime minister. Labour party rules and traditions tend to entrench their leader. No Labour prime minister has been pushed from office by his backbench MPs, and leaders in opposition have enjoyed lengthy tenures even when they are not successful in winning a general election. An unhealthy situation developed when a majority of Labour MPs expressed no confidence in Jeremy Corbyn as unfit to be prime minister. Corbyn refused to resign, saying that he was not accountable to Labour MPs but to the party members who had elected him. Only after leading Labour to two successive election defeats did Corbyn resign.

The intermittent symptoms of ill health in democratic representa-tion are very different from the potentially fatal symptoms identified in Chapter 1. Unlike would-be dictators, British governors do not take control of the media, forcing their opponents to distribute underground papers or rely on domestic or foreign social media that their undemo-cratic governors do not control. The British press is partisan but, like the House of Commons, it is divided in its partisanship and many journalists make their name by criticizing the government of the day. A govern-ment heading to dictatorship can arrest leading opposition politicians and harass or disband opposition parties. By contrast, British MPs have been recognized as a *loyal* Opposition free to criticize the government since 1826.

Elections are often held by undemocratic regimes because the outcome is certain: the rules for conducting the election are fixed to allow only one outcome. Some rules concerning the conduct of British elections have a slight bias in favour of one or another party, and this is particularly true of minor changes introduced by successive Labour and Conservative governments. However, they also have a democratic justification, such as enabling 18-year-olds to vote or equalizing the number of electors in each parliamentary constituency. These small biases do not prevent British election outcomes being uncertain and sometimes changing control of government to the surprise of the prime minister who calls the election.

Like parliamentary elections, referendums can be undemocratic plebiscites as in Napoleonic France or institutions of direct democracy, as in Switzerland (Rose 2020: Chapter 2). The conduct of British referendums is the statutory responsibility of the Independent Electoral Commission and it reviews referendum questions for clarity and impartiality. In 2016 the government proposed a virtual repeat of the question asked in the 1975 referendum on Europe: Should the United Kingdom remain a member of the European Union? After testing the question with ordinary voters and referendum stakeholders, the Commission recommended a change from the yes/no alternative as favouring a positive reply. It recommended asking voters to choose between two clear alternatives: remaining in or leaving the European Union. The government adopted the recommendation and saw its favoured outcome defeated.

9.2.2   *Direction of Government Intermittently Healthy*

Even if a new prime minister and their ministers are fast learners, they need time to be able to give informed direction to the government. Being a party leader or shadow Cabinet minister in opposition is insufficient preparation for managing a large Whitehall department, let alone supervising all of them. Of the five prime ministers since 1997 none had ever been in charge of a large organization and only two, Gordon Brown and Theresa May, were experienced in heading a large Whitehall department before becoming prime minister. Neither Tony Blair nor David Cameron had served even briefly as a junior minister and Boris Johnson's short tenure at the Foreign Office showed he preferred campaigning to developing a plan for implementing the Brexiters' vision of a global Britain.

The capacity of ministers to give direction to government is healthiest when a party wins re-election, because this provides a large pool of MPs with Whitehall experience. When the swing of the electoral pendulum brings to office a Cabinet of ministers who have never served in government it is initially infirm. This challenge arose in 1997 when Labour took office after 18 years in opposition and again in 2010 when the Conservatives took office after 13 years in opposition. Not since the 1970s has an Opposition party newly elected to government had a significant number of MPs with prior experience of holding ministerial office. British government thus rotates between a period of good health in which ministers are familiar with giving direction to government and periods of indifferent health when ministers are learning how to manage their responsibilities.

For the policymaking process to be in good health, a minister must engage with civil servants in order to combine their own political skills with the civil servants' knowledge of how to fit a new policy into existing government commitments. However, there is a tendency for ministers whose party has just won office to suspect civil servants are unsympathetic to their party because they have just spent years working for their opponents. Special political advisers can advise their minister on what will be good for the party and the minister's personal reputation, but this can create unhealthy tension with a minister's senior civil service advisers. The more experienced ministers become, the more likely they are to have a healthy relationship with civil servants, even to the point of going native, that is, evaluating a measure in Whitehall terms without considering the reaction of MPs and the media.

Early in Boris Johnson's prime ministership, there was a potentially fatal threat to a healthy relationship between ministers and civil servants when Johnson gave his authority to Dominic Cummings to build a policymaking team to formulate innovative policies and transform Whitehall. Cummings' strategy was based on Joseph Schumpeter's theory of creative destruction; he wanted to replace civil servants' analysis with computer models designed to achieve 'moon shot' goals. However, his power grab made him enemies, and after purging half a dozen leading civil servants Cummings was forced to leave Downing Street before he could put his plans into effect. Johnson sought to cauterize the wounds created by appointing officials trusted in Whitehall to co-ordinate policymaking.

Democratic accountability has been intermittently weakened by responsibility for delivering large public services being given to non-departmental public agencies and private enterprises that are not accountable to the electorate. Whitehall departments have justified doing so on grounds of economy and efficiency. In addition, this frees departments from the burden of administering high-volume routine services to hundreds of localities and millions of people nationwide. The arrangement is in satisfactory health as long as the policies that are outsourced do not run into problems for which the minister must give an account to Parliament. Given the scale of delegated public services, unwanted incidents—a fire, a rise in train fares or patients dying while queuing for hospital treatment—are inevitable. It is a symptom of bad health if ministers shuffle blame onto other public sector institutions rather than take action to remedy a problem for which they are democratically accountable.

The absence of a constitution empowering courts to enforce limits on the actions of government of the day is a chronic symptom of ill health in British democracy. Although the Supreme Court meets within sight of the Palace of Westminster, there is a consensus among MPs of all parties that it should not interfere with the activities of the government of the day. Instead, courts should be non-political, that is, confining judgements to cases that do not question the right of the government to act free of judicial constraints common in many democracies. Self-restraint has been the chief constraint on what the government does. This does not challenge the health of British democracy as long as political disputes do not arise about the government's right to do what it wants. Brexit created such challenges. When the UK Supreme Court ruled in September 2019 that the Conservative government was compelled to follow an Act of Parliament affecting its Brexit negotiations, the prime minister complied but did not consent to the court's authority. Johnson also proposed to nullify a Northern Ireland clause in an EU treaty he had signed until slapped down by the European Union.

The death of democracy occurs when the institutions of government are transformed so that autocratic rulers make public officials accountable to themselves rather than to a democratically elected parliament, a critical media or the courts. Chapter 5 documents a number of symptoms of unhealthy practices in how governments treat accountability, allowing personal staff of the prime minister and partisan advisers to give directives to civil servants and even some ministers. However, it is a mistake to regard this as an undemocratic purge, for such appointees are temporary: they come and go with the minister on whose authority they depend. There is no wholesale planting of cadres of party-loyal officials in government, as in the Soviet Union or Hitler's Third Reich. The use of rigged committees of inquiry to whitewash government actions such as Bloody Sunday and going to war in Iraq on a false prospectus is a symptom of ill health. However, the subsequent inquiries that reversed the initial whitewashes are a critical example of democracy, the capacity to correct faults.

The absence of a constitution empowering courts to enforce limits on the actions of the government of the day is a chronic symptom of ill health in British democracy. Boris Johnson's unprecedented attempt during the Brexit negotiations to ignore an Act of Parliament and an EU treaty were brazen challenges to the rule of both domestic and international law. But they were also stopped by the UK Supreme Court and by the European Commission. Johnson's appointment of a panel to undertake an innocuously named Independent Review of Administrative Law authorized to consider giving the government of the day greater freedom from judicial review of its political decisions. If it recommends weakening further the courts' role in constitutional matters, then even if this does not lead to legislation such a recommendation would, like a Sword of Damocles, hang over justices of the UK Supreme Court.

9.2.3   Challenges from Beyond Westminster

A multinational democracy is in good health as long as there is a consensus among elected national representatives that its multinational boundaries should remain unchanged. In Scotland there is currently institutionalized dissensus. Although both the UK and the devolved Scottish National Party governments accept the democratic principle of rule by the people, there is a fundamental conflict about which people can decide Scottish independence. The UK government accepts that a referendum on independence could be held once in a generation—that is, the next one should occur about 2040—to see whether majority opinion has changed since an independence referendum was held in 2014 and a majority endorsed remaining in the United Kingdom. The SNP-controlled Scottish Parliament has legislated for a second referendum to be held promptly because Scotland has been taken out of the European Union against the 2016 vote of a Scottish majority to remain in the

United Kingdom. The UK government is using its statutory powers to refuse permission for a fresh independence referendum while the SNP is relying on its electoral legitimacy to justify an independence referendum. The resulting impasse is a political ulcer that could burst.

In Northern Ireland the Good Friday Agreement is an armistice based on an arrangement inconsistent with democracy at Westminster—compulsory power-sharing between all political parties—as a price worth paying to end IRA violence. The United Kingdom's Withdrawal Agreement from the EU institutionalized an economic border on shipping goods from Great Britain to Northern Ireland and avoided creating a border between the United Kingdom's limb, Northern Ireland, and the Republic, an EU member state. This was done to prevent the revival of violence by the IRA blowing up customs posts with the Republic and shooting border guards. There is UK provision for a democratic referendum to be held on Irish unification but neither the United Kingdom nor the Irish government wants to implement it for fear that it would trigger violence by Unionists opposed to integration with the Republic or by the IRA if Irish unification failed to win a majority. The Good Friday Agreement is not a cure but a mechanism for managing the split-personality disorder in Northern Ireland politics.

Prime ministers have persistently shown a cognitive disability in weighing the power of the United Kingdom compared to that of the world's major powers. Tony Blair thought that he would be the leader of a great power by tagging along with the United States in the invasion of Iraq. David Cameron thought that the European Union and his friend 'Angie' (that is, the German chancellor Angela Merkel) would give him whatever he wanted to appease his Eurosceptic MPs. Both Theresa May and Boris Johnson claimed that leaving the European Union would produce a magical cake, that is, an agreement that allowed the United Kingdom to keep the economic benefits of membership without accepting its obligations. Their misperception brought failure to each in a different way. May and the EU agreed a compromise setting terms of relations but this failed domestically as the House of Commons rejected the compromise three times. Boris Johnson succeeded domestically in selling a deal with Brussels that increased the regulation of British exporters by creating the misperception among Conservative MPs that regaining formal sovereignty meant that the UK economy would be free of EU regulations.

Anyone wanting an evaluation of British democracy in a single number can produce it themselves by applying social science quantitative procedures to the above diagnosis. This requires deciding which attributes of democracy are important, weighing them by their importance, and evaluating each on a scale from always democratic in practice to never democratic over decades. The weighted evaluations can then be summed and divided by the number of attributes to produce a single numerical value for British democracy. The result would be numerically precise. However, the more details given to explain the substantive meaning of this numerical score, the more it is likely to read like the diagnosis of the body politic given above.

The clinical examination of the British body politic produces a bill of health that mixes both positive and negative symptoms, in keeping with an evaluation of different parts of the body politic by multiple criteria. Democratic representation is in good health with intermittent symptoms of ill health, such as the electoral system not manufacturing a parliamentary majority for the leading party at every general election. The way in which elected politicians give direction to government is intermittently in good health, varying with the skills of individual politicians to get on top of large organizations. There is a chronic risk of bad health arising from the lack of a supreme court with sufficient bite to resolve many constitutional disputes. Democratic health in both Scotland and Northern Ireland depends on both the UK government and nationalist parties co-operating while waiting for a referendum that would either maintain or break up the United Kingdom.

Unusual behaviour, such as Boris Johnson's readiness to ignore an Act of Parliament or an EU treaty, can be extrapolated into a scenario of the death of British democracy by piling unlikely assumption on unlikely assumption. However, there are far more symptoms of the resilience of British democracy that could be extrapolated to show British democracy becoming perfectly healthy by taking actions to get rid of symptoms of ill health.

9.3   Prescriptions for Treatment

Because symptoms of democratic ill health do not have a single cause, there is no big-bang prescription that can make a political system perfectly healthy all at once. Moreover, applying the remedy for what was considered one ill, for example, introducing proportional representation, would introduce another, the replacement of single-party government by a multi-party coalition that could only with difficulty be held accountable. There are a variety of piecemeal changes that could make the British body politic healthier; there are placebos that might pacify critics but achieve little else; and proposals that sound sensible may be either technically or politically impossible in the British context.

The following pages set out six technically feasible changes that could be introduced in the life of a Parliament—if the government of the day chose to do so. Some are not practical politics at the moment because they are unacceptable to the government of Boris Johnson. Yet the government of the day is only a temporary obstacle; the Conservative government's term of office expires no later than a 2024 general election. By that date, Johnson will have been in office for five and one-half years. Four of his eight Conservative predecessors since 1945 have been prime ministers for a shorter period and five have been pushed from Downing Street by their own MPs rather than by electoral defeat. After 14 years in office the Conservative government will face Opposition parties campaigning with the argument, 'It's time for a change'.

9.3.1   Feasible

Give statutory teeth to the courts to curb government abuses of power. Judges face major political difficulties in citing an unwritten Constitution as the grounds for placing restraints on government, but they can and do overrule government actions that violate Acts of Parliament. The Johnson government's panel currently evaluating judicial review may recommend the adoption of an Act of Parliament placing statutory restrictions on judicial review of government actions; this would further weaken the capacity of courts to resolve constitutional disputes. Under a different government, Parliament could adopt an Act giving courts the authority to curb government abuses of constitutional powers. The powers could codify existing conventions and, as appropriate, extend the list. If the Act included a clause stating that it could only be repealed by a referendum, this would make it politically difficult for a subsequent government to use a majority in the Commons and the Lords to loosen constraints on its powers.

Break the stalemate between the UK and Scottish governments about national self-determination by jointly agreeing conditions for a referendum on independence. The refusal of the Westminster government to accept the Scottish Parliament's demand for a referendum on independence gives the Scottish National Party a grievance it uses to mobilize more support for independence. The stalemate could be broken by negotiating a two-stage set of referendum questions that focus voters on both the principle and practical implications of change.

The Brexit process demonstrates that a referendum to leave a Union involves two steps: a decision in principle to leave and a negotiation about future relations between the divorced governments. It is technically possible to have a pair of successive referendums on an issue (Rose 2020: 22ff.). If a referendum majority endorsed the principle of Scotland leaving the United Kingdom, this would trigger the negotiation of a withdrawal agreement in which the Westminster government would, like the EU Commission, give priority to the nations remaining in the United Kingdom. A second referendum would give Scots the alternatives of confirming independence from the United Kingdom in the knowledge of the consequences or remaining in the reality of the United Kingdom. An alternative would be making home rule an additional choice in the first round. If a majority endorsed it, if only as a second choice, this would force the UK government to draft an Act of Parliament giving practical meaning to this vague term. A second referendum could then offer a choice between home rule and independence. Either two-stage referendum would not only be democratic but also offer a more informed choice than a single-stage referendum that offered the uncertainties of trusting a Westminster vow to give more powers to Scotland or a Scottish government claim that Westminster and Brussels would accommodate the wishes of an independent Scotland to have open borders with both.

Seek amendment of the EU–UK 2021 Political Agreement. Pro-Brexit campaigners won the 2016 referendum by promising future benefits from leaving the European Union. By the time of the next general election, the costs as well as the benefits will be evident to British businesses, consumers and holiday-makers. By then, the EU will have shown fresh evidence of how it responds to challenges such as the coronavirus epidemic and subsequent economic restructuring. A new European Commission and European Parliament will be in place in 2024 too. That would be an appropriate time for a new British government to start negotiations about reducing or removing costs that the 2020 agreements have imposed on both sides. Within the EU, the Republic of Ireland would have a particular stake in supporting improvements. Pro-Brexit MPs would find it difficult to oppose measures to remove specific costs their victory had imposed as long as the principle of sovereignty was respected. There would therefore be no political need for another referendum on amending the 2020 Trade and Co-operation Agreement. If the Conservative government that negotiated the 2020 agreement was worried about retaining North of England seats it won from Labour in 2019, it could itself seek beneficial amendments.

Make MPs solely responsible for the choice of their party leader. The means of removing a party leader is much healthier than the means of choosing a party leader. MPs can force a change in the leadership of their parliamentary party, even if the leader is prime minister, and voters can trigger a change at a general election or signal dissatisfaction through opinion polls. However, the current rules of the Conservative and Labour parties have taken away from MPs the power to choose a party leader. The final say is given dues-paying party members, a small fraction of a party's voters less able to judge the character of candidates than MPs. In 2019 this imposed on the electorate a choice between parties whose leaders were viewed as the lesser or greater evil. The remedy is simple: reinstate the former rules that give a party's MPs the power to choose the party leader in Parliament and, when the party is in power, the prime minister. MPs could unilaterally force this change if the candidate who finished second in a run-off vote of MPs withdrew, leaving the first-place candidate the new leader by default.

Increase Whitehall civil servants' experience of the world beyond Whitehall. Ideally, senior civil servants should combine knowledge of the world of Whitehall with the world beyond it that is affected by its policies. The current career progression of graduates recruited into the civil service straight from university gives in-depth knowledge about how Whitehall deals with problems but not how Britons deal with Whitehall's solutions. The policy process would be improved if civil servants were required to take up a temporary placement outside Whitehall before being promoted to a top position. Within the Greater London area, there are lots of council offices, hospitals and employment offices delivering Whitehall policies and financial enterprises dominating the national economy. In the North of England it is easy to learn about problems of unemployment and immigration that are not recorded in official statistics.

Increase ministerial focus on departmental policies and policymaking. Many ministers are appointed to head a department on short notice with little prior knowledge of its policies and little incentive to focus on longer-term objectives. Moreover, the governing party's election manifesto is usually short on practical details of implementing party promises. A prime minister is unlikely to accept constraints on the patronage and public relations benefits that accrue from the current system, in which departmental effectiveness is only one criterion. If the Commons committee scrutinizing their department invited each newly appointed minister to give it a detailed statement of departmental priorities, this would yield more information than partisan exchanges in parliamentary questions. Since some MPs on the committee could well have more knowledge of the department than a new minister, it would force the new appointee to get up to speed fast to answer their questions. The committee could then issue a brief report giving its own view on what the new minister ought to deal with and monitor what happens to the agenda that the minister offers.

There is no need to make prescriptions for changing the Downing Street institutions supporting the prime minister; they are sure to alter with every change of prime minister. Each prime minister enters Downing Street with his or her distinctive view of how they want to be supported. Their ideas are subject to change with fluctuations in opinion polls and domestic and international events. For example, when Boris Johnson entered Downing Street he wanted to be a leader delivering feel-good speeches. Within weeks of delivering Brexit, the coronavirus pandemic challenged Johnson to display very different skills in making policy choices based on bad news about the dynamics of the coronavirus pandemic and statistics and forecasts of its economic impact.

9.3.2   Placebos

Politicians can serve up policies that are placebos, symbolic reforms designed to soothe political pains without having a direct effect on the body politic. However, doing so takes time and political capital. Moreover, placebos may have unexpected or unwanted side effects. Two popular placebos are:

Moving civil servants out of London. Bringing the government closer to cities where more than four-fifths of the British people live is a perennially popular cry. It is a logical, even necessary complement to the idea of devolving more powers to local authorities that remain dependent on central government finance and Acts of Parliament. It overlooks the fact that at present about four-fifths of civil servants already live outside London, dealing with lower level and more routine activities. At the same time a substantial majority of senior civil servants dealing with policy issues work in London (Davies 2020). The Johnson government is talking about moving to the North of England significant policymaking functions of important economic ministries. Since the number of policymaking jobs is at most only a few hundred, the rationale for such a move is not increasing the numbers employed in the North but political symbolism. The effect of moving senior policymakers to the North of England would be to distance them from ministers whose policy intentions they serve. Moving ministers to the North of England as well would distance them from MPs, party leaders and fellow Cabinet ministers. There would also be the risk of officials resigning their posts and taking other, and often higher-paying jobs in London.

Reform of the House of Lords. There are continuing calls to replace the non-elected membership of the House of Lords with a democratically elected membership. Electing two chambers by different means creates the potential for conflict, such as that between the Senate and House of Representatives in the United States. Most active non-elected peers have knowledge of the policymaking process acquired in careers as ministers, diplomats, senior civil servants and leaders of civil society institutions. Their replacement by party nominees, for example, local councillors and unsuccessful parliamentary candidates, would have less ability to make an impact on the government of the day. Moreover, if a reformed upper chamber contained nominated candidates with specialist knowledge, this would reduce its electoral legitimacy. A reform that removed an anachronistic second chamber and weakened its members' capacity to question government would be a placebo acceptable to the government of the day. Finding a method to fill a second chamber with members who are both democratically elected and expert in government would make it better able to impose checks on the government. Awareness of this explains why both Conservative and Labour governments have rejected such a reform for more than half a century.

9.3.3   Technically Impossible, Politically Impossible or Both

Because politics is about the exercise of power, it is unrealistic to expect the government of the day to adopt measures that would limit its own power or for the Opposition to make pledges that would deny it the power that goes to the election-winner. A major reform can occasionally be adopted by a government that has not understood the consequences of what it was doing. For example, in opposition Tony Blair endorsed the principle of a freedom of information act to open up government to the people. In his memoir, Blair (2010) described himself as a stupid nincompoop for not realizing that the Act opened up the activities of the Labour government to critical journalists.

Federalism. The idea of dealing with the challenges of Scottish and Welsh nationalism by turning the United Kingdom into a federal state is logical. Australia and Canada provide examples of a parliamentary system of government that is also federal. Both these countries meet a key feature of a federal system: no part is big enough to dominate all the others. When the United Kingdom was created as a unitary multinational state in 1801, England was only 52 per cent of its population and pre-famine Ireland 33 per cent. However, today England is 84 per cent of the United Kingdom's population. In order to prevent England from having an absolute majority in making decisions about UK policies, the votes of Scotland, Wales and Northern Ireland would need to be weighted by five times more than their population. Giving Scotland, Wales and Northern Ireland representatives a veto in a federal parliament would never receive endorsements in a UK Parliament or referendum in which English votes are by far the most numerous.

A written Constitution. It is technically possible for the United Kingdom to have a written constitution, and public policy groups have produced draft constitutions that codify many existing practices and incorporate their preferred reforms (Cornford 1991). However, producing a constitution raises questions that invite political dispute (House of

Commons 2014). If the constitution were drafted by a constitutional convention, how would its members be chosen to reflect diverse stakeholders in British society? If it were drafted in Westminster, would its contents be decided by the government of the day or by an all-party parliamentary group? Would the terms of reference for the document restrict it to codifying existing practices or recommend the addition of reforms? Would a constitution require approval simply by Parliament or by a referendum as well? Would referendum endorsement require approval by a simple UK majority or by majorities in all four nations of the United Kingdom? While answers can be given to each of these questions, there is no political consensus. In the event of a crisis arising about an issue of constitutional importance, there would also be no time to produce a written constitution.

9.4 CODA

Living in a democracy gives every Briton a chance to lead their daily life free from political interference while simultaneously having social benefits from the government that increase their capacity to use their freedom (cf. Berlin 1958; Sen 1985). To evaluate the impact of democratic institutions on the lives of citizens, the 2019 European Election Survey asked people how important it is to live in a democracy. The slowness of the British government in implementing Brexit resulted in British respondents being included in the survey.

An absolute majority of Britons think it is very important to live in a democracy; only one-sixth see it as of little or no importance (Fig. 9.3). The commitment of Britons and Europeans generally to living in a democracy questions the assumption of doom-mongers of democracy that an undemocratic regime can take power without regard to the views of its citizens. The evidence suggests that any elite attempt to turn a democratic regime into a regime that infringes on the lives of ordinary people would invite mass resistance. The anti-democratic practices that Hungarian and Polish regimes have introduced have concentrated on restricting institutional checks on their own power and avoided reintroducing controls on individual lives that were pervasive in communist regimes.

The British people give three cheers for democratic principles. However, when asked to evaluate the practice of democracy, they think

Q. How important is it for you to live in a country that is governed democratically?

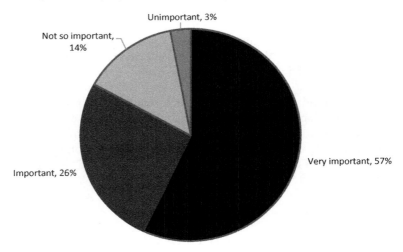

Fig. 9.3 Importance of living in a democracy (*Source* British respondents to European Election Survey 2019. Answers recorded: Very important, 9–10. Important, 7–8. Not so important, 4–6. Unimportant 0–4. Don't know omitted: 6 per cent)

it could do with improvements. This is consistent with the diagnosis and prescriptions of this study. When the time comes to hold the government of the day to account, voters sometimes confirm it in office and sometimes turn it out. Having made use of their democratic right to influence who governs, people can then make use of their freedom to engage with family, friends and work, things that contribute most to their own satisfaction with life.

9.5   A NOTE ON SOURCES

The Internet provides up-to-date information in a way that a book can never do and Internet search engines enable readers to obtain additional information from multiple sources about specific topics referred to in this book. As this book was written in lockdown, I have made use of multiple Internet sources, particularly to check my memory of dates and quotations. As some of the topics of the book are in flux, readers can find fresh news and links to background materials at www.bbc.co.uk/news/uk.

Information about the past from 1066 to Brexit can be found on many websites. The House of Commons Library provides detailed briefings and reports about a very wide range of topics covered in this book. Its papers are authoritative and non-partisan, since they are used by MPs of all parties: https://commonslibrary.parliament.uk/about-us/services/res ources/.

Information on the policies, structure and ministers of the British government is available at www.gov.uk. The website of Parliament, www. parliament.uk, contains information on current legislation and debates, and British newspapers interpret current events in the light of their particular political perspective. Biographies of current MPs and House of Lords members on the official site are complemented by Wikipedia, which contains details that politicians may choose to omit from their parliamentary accounts.

Many symptoms of the health of British politics are unwittingly revealed in quotations and guarded statements in official documents. The text gives the name, year and context that can be entered in a search engine to provide the context of quotations. Where none is given, that is usually because I have drawn on private conversations in Westminster and beyond over many decades.

Using a medical model to diagnose the condition of British democracy follows from this book's public policy focus. My neighbour, Wilfrid Card, the first professor of computer applications to diagnostic medicine in the United Kingdom, introduced me to the similarities in diagnostic medicine and political diagnosis half a century ago. The experience was broadened by publishing research on problems of social medicine in Russia with Sir Michael Marmot and colleagues at the medical school of University College London.

Articles and books written for a specialist political science audience invariably contain copious references to academic publications that discuss aspects of British politics on their own or in a comparative framework. While readers with access to university libraries can normally obtain these publications free of charge, readers without cannot. The great majority of such articles offer explanations of past events. Since this book has a different focus, the current state of British democracy, references in each chapter are kept to a minimum.

As the government of England is ten centuries old, it would have defeated the book's purpose to give a developmental account of Britain's democratization; the process is described in many books. I have published an empirical analysis of the process by which England became a modern political system in the 1850s in 'England: A Traditionally Modern Culture' (Rose 1965). An analysis of important developmental changes over the past half of the twentieth century can be found in Richard Rose, *The Prime Minister in a Shrinking World* (Rose 2001). This book picks up where these leave off.

In writing this book I can draw on personal observation of British politics for more than 65 years. This lengthy perspective has provided a guard against treating current events as permanent. Just as individual health is not a constant, so the resilience and limitations of British democracy result in symptoms of ill health and evidence of good health fluctuating.

REFERENCES

Berlin, Isaiah. 1958. *Two Concepts of Liberty: An Inaugural Lecture*. Oxford: Clarendon Press.
Blair, Tony. 2010. *A Journey*. London: Random House.
Butler, David, and Donald Stokes. 1969. *Political Change in Britain*. London: Macmillan.
Cornford, James. 1991. *The Constitution of the United Kingdom*. London: Institute for Public Policy Research.
Davies, Oliver. 2020. *Location of the Civil Service*. London: Institute of Government.
Ferrin, Monica, and Hanspeter Kriesi (eds.). 2016. *How Europeans View and Evaluate Democracy*. Oxford: Oxford University Press.
Fieldhouse, E., J. Green, G. Evans, J. Mellon, C. Prosser, H. Schmitt, and C. Van der Eijk. 2020. *Electoral Shocks: The Volatile Voter in a Turbulent World*. Oxford: Oxford University Press.
House of Commons. 2014. *A New Magna Carta?* London: House of Commons Political and Constitutional Reform Committee Proceedings, July 3.

Rose, Richard. 1965. England: A Traditionally Modern Culture. In *Political Culture and Political Development*, ed. L. Pye and S. Verba, 83–129. Princeton: Princeton University Press.

Rose, Richard. 2001. *The Prime Minister in a Shrinking World*. Oxford and Boston: Polity Press.

Rose, Richard. 2020. *How Referendums Challenge European Democracy*. London: Palgrave Macmillan.

Sen, Amartya K. 1985. *Commodities and Capabilities*. Amsterdam: North-Holland.

INDEX

© The Editor(s) (if applicable) and The Author(s), under exclusive
license to Springer Nature Switzerland AG 2021
R. Rose, *How Sick Is British Democracy?*,
Challenges to Democracy in the 21st Century,
https://doi.org/10.1007/978-3-030-73123-6

175

Printed by Printforce, the Netherlands